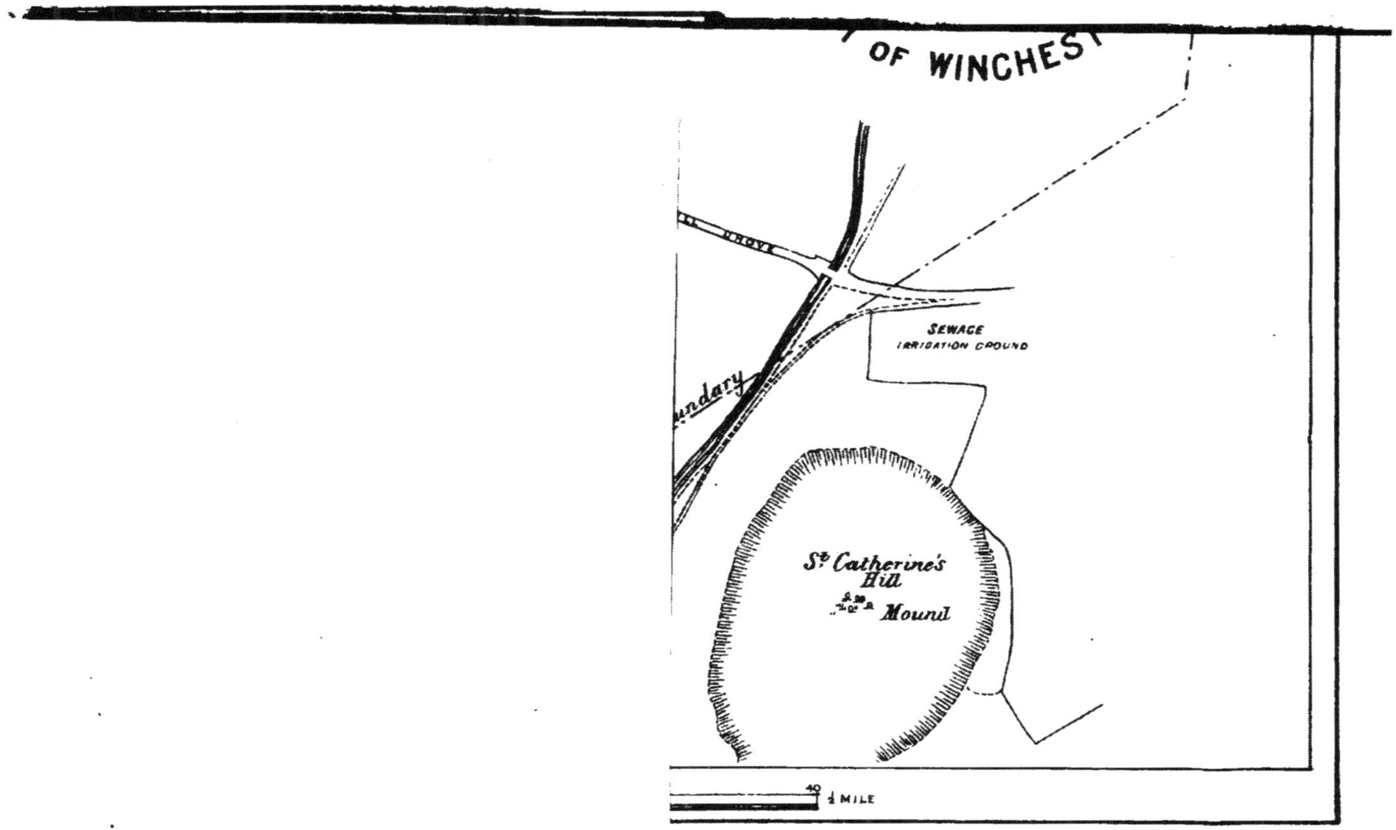

OF WINCHEST
undary
DROVE
SEWAGE
IRRIGATION GROUND
St Catherine's
Hill
Mound
40
½ MILE

WINCHESTER CATHEDRAL.

FROM ST. GILES' HILL

THE WEST FRONT

FROM THE NORTH EAST

FROM THE NORTH WEST

THE ALTAR SCREEN

FROM THE SOUTH EAST

NAVE and WEST WINDOW

THE CHOIR from ALTAR

THE NAVE LOOKING EAST

BISHOP FOX'S CHANTRY

THE NORTH TRANSEPT

CARDINAL BEAUFORT'S TOMB

GUIDE

TO

Winchester Cathedral

THE COLLEGE

ST. CROSS

KING'S CASTLE	CITY CROSS
HYDE ABBEY	WESTGATE
BISHOP'S CASTLE	GUILDHALL, &c.

MAP AND ILLUSTRATIONS.

Winchester:
WARREN & SON, PRINTERS.

Price One Shilling.
Cloth 2/-

Winchester Cathedral.

DIMENSIONS.

Extreme length, W. to E.	556 feet
,, breadth at Transepts	230 ,,
Width of each Transept	81 ,,
Nave, length of	250 ,,
,, height of	77 ,,
Nave and Aisles, breadth of	88 ,,
Choir, length of	138 ,,
Tower, height of	138 ,,
,, width of	50 ,,
Length of view on entering Western door	390 ,,

The present Establishment.

DEAN—Very Rev. John Bramston, D.D., The Deanery.

CANONS—Ven. Philip Jacob, M.A. Rev. W. Carus, M.A. Rt. Rev. Bishop F. D. Mc Dougall, D.C.L. Rev. Ernest R. Wilberforce, M.A. Ven. P. Atkinson, M.A.

MINOR CANONS—Rev. J. G. Crowdy, M.A., *Precentor.* Rev. F. T. Madge, M.A., *Librarian.* Rev. W. Mann, M.A., S.C.L. Rev. T. Marshall, M.A.

ORGANIST—George B. Arnold, MUS. DOC.

CHAPTER CLERK—F. Bowker, Esq.

NOTE.—The charter of Henry VIII recites that the reformed establishment shall consist of:—a dean, twelve prebendaries, twelve students (six at each University), twelve petty canons, twelve lay vicars, ten choristers, a master of choristers, a gospeller, a 'pisteller,' two sextons, two butlers, two cooks, one porter, two bell-ringers, twelve poor men (who had grown decayed in his majesty's service), a steward, and an auditor.

By the Act 3 & 4 Vict., c. 113, the present establishment consists of:—the dean and five canons, together with four minor canons (one of whom is precentor and one sacrist), an organist, nine lay vicars, (one of whom is master of choristers) with sixteen choristers, two vergers, three clerks, twelve bedesmen, and one porter. Honorary canons are also founded according to the Act, two being appointed in each year, they at present are twenty in number.

Hours of Divine Service.

ON SUNDAYS.—Morning Prayer, 8.30 A.M. Litany and Communion Service, 11 A.M. Evening Prayer at 4, preceded by Sermon at 3.30.

ON WEEKDAYS, at 10 A.M. and 4 P.M.

The Holy Communion is administered on Sundays and the Great Festivals at 8 and 11 A.M.

Additional Service for the Military in the Nave on Sundays at 9.30 A.M.

The Cathedral is open from 9 A.M. to 5 P.M. daily in Winter, and to 6.30 P.M. from Lady-day to September the 29th.

THE EXTERIOR.

For calm dignity and massy grandeur the exterior of Winchester will hold its own against any of our cathedrals and those who are most familiar with it will be the last to wish it, in form and outline, anything but what it is. Even the low central tower, is felt, the longer you look at it, to be the only kind of tower that would suit the immense pile whose various members it combines and harmonises; being sufficient to give dignity to the whole, without overpowering any. In estimating Winchester Cathedral as an architectural work, we must remember how very different its appearance must have been when its ponderous mass was broken by at least seven towers. In addition to the central tower, two huge towers flanked the west front, which extended 40ft. beyond the present front, and two smaller towers stood at the angles of each transept. Perhaps, also, spirelets flanked the tall, stern apse, as at Peterborough. The ground covered by the present building exceeds an acre and a half.

A.D. 1320.—The eastern Norman Apse of the main building was taken down level with the floor, leaving the crypts beneath untouched. The windows of the Presbytery Aisles, and the East Window over the Choir, together with the exterior panelling, are noble specimens of Perpendicular work. The statue on the eastern apex represents Bishop Fox resting upon his emblem, the pelican.

The orientation of the Cathedral is 23° south of the east cardinal point, which agrees with the sun-rising of none of its real or legendary dedications. No explanation of this fact is known.

A.D. 1345—1400.—The WEST FRONT was rebuilt in Perpendicular Gothic. It was commenced by Bishop Edyngton; was completed, and entrance porches added, by Bishop William of Wykeham.

The Norman front extended many more feet to the West, and was flanked by two huge and nearly square towers. There was also a court of entrance or western cloister, like those of the well-known early Christian basilicas.

The figure of a Bishop, occupying a niche in the central pinnacle on the West front, taken down during the restoration in 1860, is now placed in the Feretory. By some, it is supposed to represent St. Swithun; by others, Bishop Wm. of Wykeham, or Bishop Edyngton. The new statue represents Bishop Wm. of Wykeham.

THE STONE BALCONY, or Gallery, over the Western entrance was used by the Bishops at the Festivals in giving their benedictions to the populace.

THE INTERIOR.

'O let my due feet never fail
To walk the studious cloisters pale;
And love the high-embowed roof
With antique pillars massy proof:
And storied windows, richly dight,
Casting a dim religious light.
There let the pealing organ blow
To the full-voic'd choir below,
In service high and anthems clear,
As may, with sweetness through mine ear,
Dissolve me into extacies,
And bring all heaven before mine eyes.'

IL PENSEROSO.

Entering by the western portals, we find ourselves in one of the grandest and longest of our Cathedral Naves, where the beauty of the design divides our attention with the interest of its architectural history, and the wonderful skill with which William of Wykeham, without removing a single stone of the fabric, has transformed the rude Norman which we see in the transepts into what Mr. Fergusson calls, 'the elegance of the best age of the Pointed style.' Whether we agree with this great authority or not in regarding the Perpendicular as the best of our English styles, and this Nave as 'perhaps the most beautiful Nave either in England or elsewhere,' we cannot but be almost overwhelmed with the grandeur of the view it presents.*

THE NAVE.

A.D. 1345—1400.—The original Norman columns of the Nave were cased and adorned with Perpendicular mouldings by Bishop Edyngton, and subsequently by Bishop William of Wykeham. Cardinal Beaufort and Bishop Waynflete added many decorations to the Nave.

The nave gains a special grandeur by the vaulting shafts rising from the very floor, so that, as Woodward says, 'the eye follows them upwards tardily, as if they were more lofty than they actually are, to the capitals whence the groined roof springs.' The aisle windows have a peculiarity and beauty worthy of careful notice.

The large West Window is said to be filled with glass, collected from different parts of the building, after the destruction of the rest by the Parliamentary soldiers in 1646. Winston says these pieces are very early Perpendicular glass, and may have been placed together in the window, as we now see them, in Bishop Edyngton's time (1345-54).

Two Norman shafts near the choir screen remain as originally built. These were once hidden by the rood screen, and were not cased.

The eight westerly piers on the south side retain the Norman stonework faced with new mouldings. Norman arches remain behind the triforium wall; Norman shafts may be seen above the vaulting; and Norman flat buttresses are traceable outside between the southerly clerestory windows.

* From *The Guardian*.

Near the eastern end of the south aisle, a part of the lower extremity of a Norman shaft appears. This affords some idea how the transformation of the building from Norman to Perpendicular was effected. This shaft was probably covered by some shrine or altar work, and *its* transformation was not therefore completed.

A striking yet beautiful peculiarity is that Winchester Nave has no proper triforium—a balcony close above the Nave arches taking its place. Owing to the thickness of the Norman masonry this arrangement was unavoidable.

At Canterbury Cathedral (rebuilt for the most part about the same time as Winchester) the columns of the Nave are more slender, as there the whole fabric was pulled down.

The large iron hooks between the arches were used for suspending gorgeous tapestries during festivals.

Stone from Quarr, I.W., was used by Bishop Walkelin, (1079); and, nearly three hundred years later, stone from the same place was used by Bishop Wm. of Wykeham.

'Within the shrine of Winchester Cathedral are buried the architects who erected that most beautiful Cathedral in Europe; but not every architect is so happy as to sleep in the structure his hands have builded.'*

MONUMENTS AND CHANTRIES IN NAVE.

[The figures at the commencement of the paragraphs refer to corresponding figures on the annexed Ground Plan.]

65. BP. WILLIAM OF WYKEHAM'S CHANTRY (1367—1404) —(South Aisle). 'The Chantry of Wm. of Wykeham,' says Timbs, 'is one of the best remaining specimens of a fourteenth century monument.' It was built by himself on that part of the cruciform plan of the Cathedral, which *originally* exactly corresponded with the pierced side of the Saviour on the Cross. Here also, when a boy at School, had Wykeham attended mass. (*See Illustration.*) The following is the inscription:—

'Here, overthrown by death, lies William, surnamed Wykeham.
He was Bishop of this Church, which he repaired.
He was unbounded in hospitality, as the rich and poor can alike prove.
He was also an able politician, and a counsellor of the State.
By the colleges which he founded, his piety is made known;
The first of which is at Oxford, and the second at Winchester.
You, who behold this tomb, cease not to pray
That, for such great merits, he may enjoy everlasting life.'

* *Ward Beecher.*

WILLIAM OF WYKEHAM'S CHANTRY.

5. The early Norman Font—(North Aisle)

Rev. C. Collier, M.A., in his 'Remarks on the Font in Winchester Cathedral,' alludes to similar fonts at Eastmeon, St. Michael's, Southampton, and Littleton, which he attributes to the same workmen, all being referable to the earlier Norman period, and probably to the time of Bp. Walkelin. On the Font, a Church of Norman character is represented, but the figures are dressed in the Anglo-Saxon manner. The staff in the hand of the principal figure is that of a bishop, the crook being turned *outwards*, that of an abbot inwards. The carvings on the side of the Font refer to incidents in the life of St. Nicholas, Bp. of Myra, who died A.D. 342, and whose remains were in 1087, reburied at Bari, in Italy. Creasy states that, when at Bari, he made a drawing of a stone tablet placed against the Church of *St. Nicholas*, containing *precisely* the same legend. The four incidents sculptured are:—

(1) St. Nicholas of Myra (the patron of children), by presenting dowers, saves three virgins from the disgrace to which the poverty of their father, a nobleman, would have exposed them. For want of space the nuptials of the third daughter are not represented.

(2) Incidents in the Saint's visit to the Holy Land:—The stilling of a storm; the restoration to life of a seaman who had fallen from a mast; and the healing of sick in Alexandria.

(3) St. Nicholas saving the lives of three young men condemned to death by the prefect Eustachius.

(4) A miracle ascribed to St. Nicholas after his death: the restoration of a child who had fallen, with a golden cup, into the sea on the voyage to Myra.

The ornaments on the top of the Font are doves, emblematical of the Holy Ghost, which appear breathing in phials, surmounted by crosses. On the sides of the Font, doves are repeated in various attitudes, together with a salamander, emblematical of fire, and in allusion to the passage in the gospel of St. Matthew, 'He shall baptise you with the Holy Ghost and with fire.'

'The Holy Spirit, the change from unregeneracy to regeneracy, and the sustenance of the regenerate spirit, are plainly typified by the beaked and clawed birds and animal, the doves, the grapes, and the vessels surmounted by the Cross.'—*Woodward*, p. 49.

61. Bp. Edyngton's Chantry (1345—1366)—(near steps to the Choir)—is the *earliest* of the six remaining separate chantries. The chantries of Edyngton, Wykeham, Beaufort, Waynflete, Fox, and Gardiner, severally afford striking examples of architectural detail, extending from the early Perpendicular to the Renaissance. Edyngton's Chantry was in some parts necessarily altered on the completion of the transformation of the Nave. It is recorded that Edyngton declined the appointment as Archbishop of Canterbury, saying, 'If Canterbury is the higher rack, Winchester is the better manger.' He was the first Bishop of Winchester who received the Order of the

Garter, which was granted to him by Edward III. The following inscription on the tomb remains:—

'William, born at Edington, is buried here.
He was a bountiful bishop, and Winchester was his see.
Ye, who pass by, remember him in your prayers.
He was discreet and mild; of great erudition;
A watchful guardian of the English nation;
A tender father and a protector of the poor.
This holy prelate died on the eighth of October,
M. thrice C. with LXV. and I. [1366] being the year.'

64. *Cheere's* Monument to Bp. Willis (1734)—(South Aisle)

Milner, after praising its execution, says the sculptor died of vexation at the blunder he had committed in placing the head to the west.

8. Colonel Boles (Royalist)—(north-east corner, left side of first steps leading up to the Choir)

'*A Memoriall.*—For this Renowned Martialist *Richard Boles*, of the Right Worshipful Family of the *Bolses* in *Linkhorne Shire*, Collonell of a Ridgment of Foot of 1300, who for his gracious King *Charles* the First did wounders at the Battle of *Edge-hill.* His last Action, to omit all others, was at *Alton*, in this County of *Southampton*, was surprised by five or six thousand of the Rebels; which caused him, there quartered, to fly to the Church with near four score of his Men, who then fought them six or seaven hours; and then the Rebells breaking in upon him, He slew with his Sword six or seven of them, and then was slain himself, with sixty of his men about him.—1641.

'His gracious Sovereign hearing of his Death gave him his high commendation, in that passionate Expression,

'*Bring me a Moorning scarf, I have lost
One of the best Commanders in the Kingdome.*

'*Alton* will tell you of that famous Fight
Which this Man made, and bade this world good night;
His vertuous Life fear'd not Mortalyty—
His Body must, his Vertues cannot die.
Because his blood was there so nobly spent:
This is his Tombe, that *Church* his Monument.

*Richardus Boels Wiltoniensis in Art. Mag.
Composuit posuitq: Dolens.* An. Dni. 1689.'

⊙ Edward Cole erected this monument during his life, but dying during the Stuart civil wars, no inscription was ever placed on it.

2. The Two Brothers of Avington—(North Aisle)

'A Union of Two Brothers from Avington. The Clerks Family were Grandfather, Father, and Son, successively Clerks of the Privy Seal. William, the Grandfather, had but two sons, both Thomas's, their wives both Amy's, and their heirs both Henry's, and the heirs of Henry's both Thomas's. Both their wives were inheritrixes, and both had two sons and one daughter, and both their daughters issueless. Both of Oxford, both of the Temple, both officers to Queen Elizabeth and our noble King James. Both Justices of the Peace, both agree in arms, the one a Knight, the other a Captain. *Si Quæras Avingtonum, Petas Cancellum. Impensis Thomæ Clerk of Hide.* 1662.'

3. Monumental brass in Memory of Jane Austen, authoress—(North Aisle)

'In memory of JANE AUSTEN, youngest daughter of the late Rev. George Austen, formerly Rector of Steventon, in this County. She departed this life on the 18th of July, 1817, aged 41, after a long illness supported with the patience and hope of a Christian. The benevolence of her heart, the sweetness of her temper, and the extraordinary endowments of her mind, obtained the regard of all who knew her, and the warmest love of her intimate connexions. Their grief is in proportion to their affection; they know their loss to be irreparable, but in their deepest affliction they are consoled by a firm, though humble hope, that her charity, devotion, faith, and purity have rendered her soul acceptable in the sight of her Redeemer.'

4. Mrs. Montagu, Founder of the Blue Stocking Club, and Chimney Sweepers' Friend—(near the Font)

'Here lies the body of Elizabeth Montagu, daughter of Matthew Robinson, Esq., of West Layton, in the county of York, who, possessing the united advantages of beauty, wit, judgment, reputation, and riches, and employing her talents most uniformly for the benefit of mankind, might be justly deemed an ornament to her sex and country. She died on the 25th of August, 1800, aged 81.' The death of an infant son is also recorded.

THE BRONZE FIGURES OF JAMES I AND CHARLES I—(on either side of Western Doors). The following is extracted from mutilated *Record in Exchequer*:—

'To Hubert le Seur, in full of 340 li for 2 statues in brasse, ye one of his late Majestie, and ye other of our now Soveraigne Lo: King Charles . . 170:0:3.

'More to him 40 li for carrying and erecting 2 figures at Winchester.

Hubert le Seur, the sculptor mentioned in the above extract, was the pupil of John of Bologna, and settled in this country in 1628. He was much employed by Charles the First. The Equestrian Statue of that Monarch, at Charing Cross, and a bust of him at Stourhead, were Le Seur's work, as were the Bronze Statue of the Earl of Pembroke, presented to the University of Oxford, and a recumbent figure of the Earl of Portland on a tomb in the north-east Chapel of Winchester Cathedral.

THE NORTH TRANSEPT.

The ancient grandeur and massiveness of the North Transept should be carefully observed.

Against the wall, at the extremity of the North Transept, are traces of a colossal figure of St. Christopher carrying Christ. This explains that the transepts were intended to be plastered and decorated. The flat ceiling was placed in 1818.

13. CHAPEL OF HOLY SEPULCHRE contains very effective frescoes of XIII century, representing the Passion of our Lord. On the outer wall is a Tablet to Mrs. Trench, mother of present Archbishop of Dublin. (Organ over.)

'The path to its altar has been, so to speak, the pathway to the other world to thousands of men for a thousand years.'

THE CHOIR.

A.D. 1296.—THE CARVED STALLS in the Choir added. They are of Norwegian oak, and very beautiful in design.

The desks and stools in front of the upper range, bear initials of Bp. Gardiner, Dean Kingsmill, and Henry VIII; date 1540.

A.D. 1520.—THE PULPIT, also the SOUTH CHAPEL in South Transept, were erected by Prior Silkstede.

A.D. 1524.—THE REREDOS, together with the vaulting, and side screens of Presbytery, and the east front, erected. The Reredos was commenced by Cardinal Beaufort and completed by Bishop Fox and Prior Silkstede.

ITS DETAIL.—The Reredos at Winchester, an excellent specimen of Perpendicular work, is executed in a fine, white, soft stone; its elaborately canopied niches, pierced and crocketted pinnacles, pilaster buttresses, and centre projecting canopy, are surmounted, at a height reaching nearly to the corbels, with a triple frieze of running leaves, Tudor flowers, and quatrefoils. This Reredos is considered of the same type as that at Christchurch Abbey and St. Albans, but its dimensions are greater. Its restoration was carried out with remarkable fidelity to the original work. The back is closely panelled in the upper part, and the lower part is richly decorated. No description could do justice to the beauty and effect of the whole work.* On the spandrils of the doors, on either side of the altar, are the history of the Annunciation on the one side, and of the Visitation on the other, carved in basso relievo, and coloured, as fresh as when executed in the time of Bishop Fox. Milner describes its exquisite workmanship as being as magnificent as this or any other nation can exhibit.

* See Woodward's *History of Winchester*, p. 60.

Before the restoration of 1818, a prodigious wooden canopy, with wonderful Jacobean ornaments, and much gilding, covered all the middle part of this exquisite Reredos.

THE PRESBYTERY VAULTING.—Amongst the devices carved on the bosses of the Presbytery vaulting, Milner notices 'the arms and badges of the families of Lancaster and Tudor, the arms of Castile, of Cardinal Beaufort, and even of the very sees held successively by Bishop Fox. The part of the vaulting from the altar to the east window, bears none but pious ornaments: the several instruments of the Saviour's passion, including St. Peter's denial, and the betrayal in the Garden of Gethsemane, the faces of Pilate and his wife, of the Jewish high priest, with the Cross, crown of thorns, nails, hammer, pillar, scourges, reed, sponge, lance, sword with the ear of Malchus upon it, lanthorn, ladder, cock, dice, etc., which are deservedly commended for the variety and originality of their designs.'

The altar rails are of the time of Charles I, and the altar books, in black letter, were the gift of Charles II.

WEST'S PICTURE of the 'Raising of Lazarus,' was purchased by Dean Ogle in the latter part of the last century.

THE FERETORY, or Capitular chapel, is immediately behind the altar, and communicates with the sanctuary. Here the magnificent shrine of St. Swithun, of solid silver, gilt and garnished with precious stones, the gift of King Edgar, used to be kept, except on the festivals of the saint, when it was exposed to view on the altar, or before it.

From the platform behind the Reredos may be observed the admirable connection of Fox's new with De Lucy's earlier work. The original south-east pier having failed, the present erection differs from the composite pier on the north-east side.

Of the ANCIENT ALTAR PLATE, Jewels, etc.:—

ETHELWOLD, Bishop of Winchester, A.D. 980, in a famine, sold all the rich vessels and ornaments in the church at that time, to relieve the poor with bread; and said, 'There was no reason that the dead temples of God should be sumptuously furnished, and the living temples suffer penury.'—BACON'S *Apophthegms.*

CANUTE, after rebuking the flattery of his courtiers at Southampton, placed his crown over the crucifix on the High Altar, and also presented a large crucifix set with jewels.—A.D. 1032.

Images of the Saviour on the Cross, with the Blessed Virgin on the one side and St. John on the other, were also presented by Bishop De Blois, and were composed of pure gold studded with jewels.

AMONGST THE TREASURES relinquished to King Henry VIII were:—The nether part of the High Altar, of plate of gold, garnished with stones, the front above being of broidery work and pearls, and above that a table of images of silver and gilt garnished with stones; above the altar a great cross and image of plate of gold, similarly garnished; in the body of the church a great cross and images of Christ, Mary, and John, being of plated silver, partly gilt (which was the gift of Stigand,* whilst Bishop of Winchester); St. Swithun's shrine of plate silver with many other shrines; relics of saints covered with plate of gold; crosses, chalices, and other church utensils, vestments, etc., in almost countless store, including the splendid gifts of Canute above mentioned, and a book of the four Evangelists written all with gold, and the outer side of plate of gold.

A.D. 1525.—THE EAST WINDOW (over the Reredos) inserted by Bishop Fox.

Winston says, 'in point of execution it is as nearly perfect as painted glass can be. In it the shadows have attained their proper limit. It was at this period that glass painting attained its highest perfection as an art. When perfect, the glass in this part of the Cathedral might have stood a comparison with the finest continental examples.'

In the lowest compartments are figures of St. Swithun, St. Paul with his sword, St. Peter, St. Malichias with his name on the border of mantle, and others unknown. Above is the figure of St. Ethelwold with two prophets, (one of whom, from the circular legend round his head—'The earth hath quaked, the heavens have been moved,'—is Joel, and in the topmost compartments are figures of the Saviour, the Blessed Virgin, and St. Bartholomew. Angels bearing the arms of the See of Winchester, of Bishop Fox, together with his motto, 'Est Deo Gratia,' and angels holding trumpets, are stained in the richest colours.

A.D. 1350.—The PRESBYTERY piers and arches were erected by Bishop Edyngton in the Decorated style.

A.D. 1510.—Bishop Fox erected the outer walls of the Presbytery, the windows of which are fine specimens of Perpendicular.

* Stigand, a Saxon by birth, was Bishop of Winchester and Archbishop of Canterbury concurrently, 1047-70. He was also chaplain to Queen Emma. He was deposed by William the Conqueror, as were most of the other Saxon Bishops, and died a prisoner in Winchester Castle. All his large property was confiscated to the crown, excepting the silver plate he had dedicated for the adornment of Winchester Cathedral.

THE MORTUARY CHESTS—(over the side screens of the Choir). Bishop Henry de Blois, who erected the former side screens of the Choir (1129—1171), collected the bones of kings and saints who had been buried in the crypts, on whose monuments were no inscriptions, and placed them in leaden chests. Bishop Fox (1524) placed these bones in the present six chests. Few things in this noble Cathedral produce a deeper impression on the mind of the stranger than these Mortuary Chests.

These chests were examined in the year 1797, by H. Howard, Esq., of Corby Castle, and other gentlemen:—The first chest from altar-screen, on south, inscribed Edred, contains many thigh bones and two skulls. *

Second chest, south, inscribed Edmund, contains five skulls and three or four thigh bones. One of the skulls belonged to a very old man, another to an old person; these, therefore, might have belonged to Wina and Alwin.

Third chest, south, and first from pulpit on north, bear the names of Canute, Rufus, Emma,† Wina, Alwin, Stigand. Neither contains any skull, but are full of thigh and leg bones; one set in third chest is smaller and weaker than the rest. This with supernumary skull in second chest from pulpit, inscribed Egbert and Kenulph, might have belonged to Queen Emma.

The second from the pulpit also contains three skulls, one very small; one thigh bone, wanting a fellow, is very stout, and measures nearly twenty inches long; but two leg bones (one rather deformed) and two hip bones belonging to this body answer exactly. There are also two thigh bones and two leg bones that pair, so that, with exception of the third skull, these may be the bones of the aforesaid kings.

Third chest from pulpit, inscribed Kinegils and Adulphus, contains two skulls and two sets of thigh and leg bones. From a measurement of the skulls and thighs, it appeared they were about ordinary size. The skulls in the chests are twelve, which is the number of inscribed names on the chests.

In 1845, when these chests were inspected, nothing new was discovered; but, when in 1873 these chests were examined by the Rev. C. Collier, M.A., only *eleven* skulls were found, namely:—In the first chest south from the altar, as given above, two skulls; in the second, four; in the third, none. In the first chest north from the pulpit, were no skulls; in the second, three; in the third, two.

* In Catholic times only the larger bones of saints were washed with wine and water and enshrined. The other bones, with chalice, rings, funeral clothes, etc., were always left in the original tomb.

† Earl Godwin, Emma's persecutor, was also buried in this Cathedral.

VAULTING UNDER TOWER.—The present Belfry was made, in 1634, by filling in the original choir-lantern of the Tower with wooden vaulting, ornamented with the arms, initials, and devices of Charles I, his consort, and the Prince of Wales; the arms of Scotland and Ireland, of Archbishop Laud, Bishop Curle, and Dean Young; also medallion of the royal pair, with faces in profile and legend round; in the centre is an emblem of the blessed Trinity, around which is the chronogram,—

sINT DoMUs hUjUs pII reges nUtrItII regInæ nUtrICes pIæ. May pious kings be the nursing fathers, and pious queens the nursing mothers of this church.

The larger letters are painted red. If these are picked out and arranged, the numerals MDC.VVVVV.IIIIIIII, equal to 1634, shew the date of the work.

The piers of the present Tower are the largest in England in proportion to the span of their arches. The tilted arches opening to the Transepts are strikingly narrow compared with those opening to the Nave and Chancel. The broad span of the latter arches gives uniqueness to the Choir, and affords a complete view, from the west, of the Presbytery and Reredos.

The re-opening of the lantern by the removal of this vaulting has been suggested. The inside Norman stonework above the vaulting is richly carved.

19. HARDICANUTE, the last Danish monarch—(north side near the Altar). His body was brought from Lambeth for interment. On the monument is the figure of a ship. The inscription is—

Qui jacet hic regni sceptrum tulit Hardicanutus, Emmae Cnutonis gnatus est, et ipse fuit. Ob. A.D. M.XLI.

A.D. 1202.—THE EASTERN PORTION OF THE CATHEDRAL (*beyond* the Presbytery Aisles,) called the Processional Aisles, was erected in the Early English style by Bishop GODFREY DE LUCY.

These Aisles are a very *early* specimen of Early English, and the details are of great beauty. They are said to have served as a model to the designer of Salisbury Cathedral.

Hereford Cathedral affords one of the earliest examples of these low-roofed procession Aisles. The Winchester Aisles are by far the most extensive.

The pavement contains many of the original chased and ornamented tiles which have been preserved to the present day.

39. The beautiful EDWARDIAN ARCADE—(back of Reredos)—with nine canopies, above the ancient entrance to the Crypts, well deserves notice. This vault-entrance is usually termed the 'Holy Hole.' Above it is the following inscription :—

Corpora Sanctorum sunt hic in pace sepulta—
Ex meritis quorum fulgeri miracula multa.

The bodies of different saints are here buried in peace—
Through whose merits many miracles shine forth. *

MONUMENTS IN THE EASTERN AISLES.

35. CARDINAL BEAUFORT'S CHANTRY—(1405—1447). By many, the chantry of this once enormously wealthy prelate is thought to be unrivalled. Around the tomb was an inscription,† part of which Godwin states to have been—

'TRIBULARER SI NESCIREM MISERICORDIAS TUAS.'
I should be in anguish did I not know Thy mercies.

Britton says that in his time 'a horse load of the pinnacles in the canopy had fallen down.' The figure represents Beaufort in the proper dress of a cardinal—the scarlet cloak and hat, with depending cords each of ten knots. The chantry has since been repaired. (*See Illustration.*)

33. BP. WAYNFLETE'S CHANTRY. This bishop (1447—1486) was the founder of Magdalene College, Oxford. The extreme beauty and delicacy of the canopy should be noticed. No inscription was ever found. The head of the figure had been so badly repaired, that, at the recent restoration, a new head was substituted. The figure is vested in full pontificals of mitre, crozier, casula, stole, maniple, tunicle, rochet, alb, amice, sandals, and gloves. The hands are clasped, enclosing between

* In the year 1789 an attempt was made, in the presence of the author, to gain an entrance into the Holy Hole; but, upon removing the masonry which closes the present entry, the crown of the arch above was found to have been purposely destroyed, and the whole passage and vault to be so entirely choked with rubbish, that there was a necessity of abandoning the undertaking.—*Milner.*

† Of the brass torn from violated monuments might have been built a house as strong as the brazen towers in old romances.—*Timbs.*

Cardinal Beaufort's Chantry, Winchester Cathedral.—A. D. 1447.

them a heart, the *sursum corda* of the Liturgy, 'Lift up your hearts; We lift them up unto the Lord.'

42. BISHOP FOX'S CHANTRY—(south of Altar)—1500—1528, though not the best in general effect, is the most elaborate, and at one time all the arches were filled with stained glass. Blind some years before his death, he was daily led for meditation to the small oratory attached to his chantry. The groining in the fifty-five niches is different in each of them. Over the altar is the following:—

'O SACRUM CONVIVIUM IN QUO CHRISTUS SUMITUR.'
O sacred banquet in which Christ is received.

He was the founder of Corpus Christi College, Oxford.

20. BISHOP GARDINER'S CHANTRY—(north-east side of Altar)—1531—1555. Britton calls its style 'bad Italian and bad English.' The head of the emaciated figure of this prelate, placed in a long niche on the outside has been cut off by some Reformers, and the very pavement torn away out of hatred to this 'hammer of heretics.' His remains were, however, preserved from indignity by the Catholics, who placed a skull and bones over the outside of his tomb, representing them as Gardiner's. No tomb can now be traced, but over the back of the altar are figures representing the Law and the Gospel, or Justice and Mercy. In this chantry may be seen the base of one of the piers of the old Norman Presbytery.

32. The Tomb of WILLIAM RUFUS—(second central tomb in front of Lady Chapel)

King Rufus was buried under the Tower of Winchester Cathedral, 'many looking on and few grieving.'

On the occasion of this tomb being opened, and removed from the Choir, in August, 1868, the articles found consisted of the greater part of a human skeleton, fragments of lead coffin, and remains of cloth lining of same, red cloth, cloth of gold, and seven gold braids of Norman pattern, three kinds of muslin and other fabrics, a turquoise, an ivory griffin's head, fragments of small wands, and remains of a weapon, besides some small pieces of cork, broken nutshells, small twigs, etc. Dr. F. W. Richard's opinion was that the remains clearly indicated that some Norman of rank had been interred there about the commencement of the 12th century, and that if absolute certainty could not be arrived at, there was strong probability in favour of the old and general belief that the remains were in truth those of William Rufus.

Gale says, 'In the tomb of William Rufus, which was broken open by the rebels during the civil wars, was found the dust of that king, some relics of cloth of gold, a large gold ring, and a small silver chalice.'

38. PRIOR SILKSTEDE—(1524). In this tomb were found the complete remains of a human body, clothed in black serge, with 'funeral boots' yet adhering to the bones of feet. The inner tomb was of stone 'similar to that used in Bishop Fox's chapel.' It is not improbable that the remains were Silkstede's, and that they had been removed hither from his chapel.*

23. BISHOP PETER DE RUPIBUS—(north side of Processional Aisles)—was appointed Chief Justice of England, and on the death of John, guardian of the infant king, Henry III, and Regent of the kingdom. He went on a pilgrimage to the Holy Land; was Grand Master of the Freemasons from 1216, and died at Farnham Castle, June 9th, 1238.

40. PRIOR WILLIAM DE BASING (1295).

Hic jacet Willielmus de Basing, quondam Prior istius ecclesiae cujus, animae propitietur Deus, et qui pro anima ejus oraverit, tres annos ex quinquaginta dies indulgentiae percipiet.

Here lies William de Basing, who was formerly prior of this church, to whose soul God be merciful; and whosoever prays for the same, shall obtain three years and fifty days indulgence.

26. Chapel of Guardian Angels. (Bishop Orlton's Chantry) —(1345). There is no memorial of this Bishop existing.

30. BISHOP DE LANGTON'S CHANTRY. He died of plague A.D. 1500.

The vine is here beautifully carved in oak springing from a tun, indicative of his See, Winton. Bishop Langton's motto, 'Laus tibi Christi,' is also frequently repeated.

25. The heart of Bishop Ethelmar (removed from its original position), body buried in Paris, 1261. His violence and

* *Woodward*, p. 37.

rapacity caused his banishment, but he seems to have expressed his desire of returning by ordering his heart to be conveyed to this Cathedral.

22. WILLIAM SYMONDS (Founder of Christ's Hospital)—(north wall of Processional Aisles beyond Presbytery)

> ' Here lieth William Symonds, Gentleman,
> Of Winchester twice Maior and Alderman,
> Alice his wief lyes bvried by his side,
> The one in Iune, in Ivly the other died.
> On the 10th day 1601 she,
> On the 27th day 1616 he.
> His merit doth enheritt life and famé,
> For whilst this City stands Symond his name
> In alle men's harts shall never be forgotten
> For poores prayers rise when flesh lyes rotten.'

'In June, 1766, some workmen repairing Winchester Cathedral discovered a monument, wherein was contained the body of Canute. It was remarkably fresh, had a wreath or circlet round the head, and several other ornaments, such as gold and silver bands. On his finger was a ring, in which was set a remarkably fine stone; and in one of his hands was a silver penny.'*

THE LADY CHAPEL.

A.D. 1470—1524.—The LADY CHAPEL, extreme end of, added to Bishop de Lucy's work, by Priors Hunton and Silkstede.

In this Chapel was celebrated the marriage of Queen Mary with Philip of Spain, in July, 1554. The chair in which she sat on the occasion is now placed in the Chapel of the Guardian Angels. The Cathedral was richly hung with arras and cloth of gold. Bishop Gardiner officiated, and was the only person who afterwards dined with the royal pair at Wolvesey.

On the vault of this chapel, round the two centre keys, one representing the Almighty, the other the Blessed Virgin, note the following characters and rebuses: the letter *T*, the syllable *Hun*, the figure of a *ton*, for *Thomas Hunton*, and figure *I* for *Prior*. Next observe the letter *T*, the syllable *Silk*, a *steed* or horse, and figure *I* for *Thomas Silkstede*, Prior.

The wood carving in this and the next Chapel is very beautiful.

* *Archæologia*, vol. iii, p. 890.

REMAINS OF CURIOUS OLD WALL PAINTINGS OF MIRACLES IN THE LADY CHAPEL,* ADDED BY PRIOR SILKSTEDE, 1489, REPRESENTING :--

1.† Miracle of image of Virgin bending its finger, so as to prevent a young man taking off a ring (given him by his lady-love), which he had placed on the image that it might not be lost or injured while he played at ball. By this the young man was won to the monastic life.

2. Protection and honour conferred by the Virgin on an ignorant priest, who knew and could sing only one mass, which was in honor of her.

3. Prior Silkstede kneeling before Virgin, saying, 'Benedicta tu in mulieribus.' Beneath is the following :—'Prior Silkstede also caused these polished stones, O Mary, to be ornamented at his expense.'

4. Jew-boy, after receiving the Eucharist, thrown into a furnace by his father (a refiner), but delivered from the flames by the Virgin.

5. Famous portrait of the Virgin (painted by St. Luke), carried in procession by Pope Gregory to allay a fearful pestilence. During the procession the destroying angel is seen sheathing his sword.

6. A widow receives back her son who had been kidnapped, and thereupon restores the silver image of the child Jesus, which she had taken from the image of the Virgin on losing her son.

7. Virgin assisting a woman taken ill while on pilgrimage.

8. Virgin enables boys, with ease, to raise that which strong men could not.

9. Nun brought to life to confess a sin not confessed before death. [Note peculiar nimbus on the head of Christ.]

10. Virgin saves a monk from drowning, and from two evil spirits with instruments of torture for one who had lived an immoral life.

11. Two Brabançons seized by devils and killed for throwing stones at an image of the Virgin.

12. Deliverance at sea afforded by the Virgin.

13. Mass of the Virgin celebrated by Christ himself, with saints and angels, on an occasion when the priest was unable to do so.

14. St. John's (of Damascus) arm restored: thereby establishing his innocence of having corresponded with unbelievers.

15. Virgin delivering from the gallows a thief who had always venerated her.

16. Virgin commanding the burial of a clerk of irreligious life in consecrated ground, because he had been her votary.

17. Virgin assisting a painter to paint the devil 'as ugly as he knew him to be,' in spite of all the devil could do to prevent him from completing it.

* See Carter's *Specimens of Sculpture and Painting*.

† Commencing from south side near the Altar.

18. 'The Annunciation'—over door, which formerly led to a particular sacristy. Traces of the door may be seen outside.

19. How, by praying to the Virgin, a robber-knight was delivered from the clutches of the devil (defaced). 20 to 24 much defaced.

THE SOUTH TRANSEPT.

THE WILBERFORCE MEMORIAL—(Middle of the South Transept)—consists of a life-sized effigy of the Bishop, sculptured in Derbyshire alabaster, wearing his mitre and cope, with pastoral staff lying on an alabaster plinth, under which is a slab of red Belgian marble, moulded with the inscription on its edge as follows:—'*Samuel Wilberforce, nuper Wintoniensis pridem Oxoniensis episcopus. 1° die mensis Septembrii, A.S. mdcccv. natus, in fide Christi decessit xix° die mensis Julii, A.S. mdccclxxiii.*' This slab is supported on the shoulders of six kneeling angels in white alabaster, delicately draped and in the act of rising. The floor on which they kneel is of very choice brecciated marble, and the platform is elevated by two stone steps, at the angles of which are couchant lions in yellow magnesian limestone, sculptured after early examples. Over the whole is a rich canopy supported as follows:—At the four angels are substantial piers of magnesian limestone, in single blocks, carved out of the solid, of which are the four virtues—Faith, Hope, Justice, and Prudence, standing on ornamental bases with enriched canopies over. At the sides of these piers are placed—two to each—shafts of rich red Cork marble of most elaborate workmanship, being twisted, after an ancient fragment belonging to the Cathedral, somewhat similar to those in the shrine of Edward the Confessor. The columns supporting the arcading between the piers are of Greek green marble, identical with the verde antique. The columns and piers have rich Early English carved capitals in magnesian limestone, their bases also being carved, and in the same material. The canopy, of fine oolite stone, consists of eight arches, with crocketted gables, three on each side and the two at the ends, the side ones being surmounted by very elaborately carved finials of foliage and birds, like the famous ones on Archbishop Grey's monument in York Cathedral. The spandrels of the gables are filled in with delicate Early English foliage, the label terminations being heads of bishops; while at the angles are angels holding the sun and moon, suggested by the text—'Let there be lights in the firmament of the heavens.' The end gables are surmounted by rich floriated crosses. In the spandrel of the western one are carved the arms of the See of Winchester, impaling those of Wilberforce, surrounded with the Garter (of which Order he was prelate), over the whole being placed the mitre. The eastern gable is filled with the bishop's private arms, surmounted by his crest, the labels to these gables being terminated with angels holding thuribles in the act of censing. The roofs are enriched with scaling after the pattern of that to Queen Eleanor's monument in Westminster Abbey, and a perforated cresting of Early English foliage runs along the ridges. The canopy has groined vaulting, with moulded ribs, delicate foliated bosses being carved at the intersections. In the angles of the external roof are pedestals on which are four statues of the archangels. The architectural design, with all details, is by Sir George Gilbert Scott, R.A., the effigy being the work of Mr. H. H. Armstead, A.R.A. The architectural portions, with their sculptures and carvings, including the supporting angels, have been executed by Messrs. Farmer and Brindley, of London.*

50. VENERABLE CHAPEL (used as Vestry by Minor Canons.) It is supposed that formerly the Blessed Sacrament used to be kept here for the benefit of the sick, and for private communion. (Note iron work.)

51. PRIOR SILKSTEDE'S CHAPEL. (Note tracery of screen and lock.)

52. IZAAK WALTON—(in Silkstede's Chapel, South Transept) —'The Prince of Fishermen,' author of the *Lives of Donne, Hooker*, etc. (floor slab).

* From *The Hampshire Chronicle.*

'Here resteth the body of
MR. IZAAK WALTON,
Who dyed the 15th of December,
1683.
Alas! Hee's gone before,
Gone, to returne noe more.
Our panting Breasts aspire
After their aged Sire,
Whose well-spent Life did last
Full ninety Years, and past.
But now he hath begun
That which will nere be done,
Crown'd with eternall Blisse,
We wish our Souls with his.
Votis modestis sic flêrunt liberi."*
Thus with modest vows his children wept.

53. ANCIENT CALEFACTORY for preserving fire for the thuribles or censers.

54. ENTRANCE LOBBY. Wooden bench supposed to be coeval with transept itself.

55. ANCIENT STAIRCASE by which the Monks descended from adjoining Monastery to midnight Service. It now gives access to the Library.

THE CATHEDRAL LIBRARY (over the Dark Cloister) contains a collection of from three to four thousand volumes, principally on Divinity, the larger part of them the gift of Bishop Morley. Besides the books there are some exceedingly rare MSS. including *The Vulgate* (12th century) in three volumes, imperial folio, with splendid illuminations, and in good preservation†; Bede's *Ecclesiastical History* (11th century); a rare

* Bishop Ken is said to have written this inscription.

† It appears that for some years this book was lost, but was recognized at Lincoln Cathedral by a monk from Winchester, after which it was restored to its owners.

The story of Hugh of Overton (afterwards Bishop of Lincoln) and his conduct with regard to the manuscript:—King Henry II founded the Abbey of Witham, in Somerset, and appointed Hugh its Prior in 1173. After completing the buildings and filling them with an orderly brotherhood, Hugh began eagerly to seek for manuscripts, which the brethren might spend their time in copying, desiring most anxiously a complete copy of the Scriptures. One day, lamenting to the king the dearth of books, Henry gave him ten marks to buy parchment, promising himself to supply the want of a complete copy of the Bible. Henry had throughout endeavoured to provide for his Abbey at the least possible cost, and hearing of a splendidly

MS. copy of *The Promptorium Parvulorum*, etc.; also the *Chapter Book* from 1553 to 1600. Some have chains still attached to their covers.

The Dean and Chapter have in their possession a pastoral wooden staff, taken from Fox's tomb in 1820, and original Anglo-Saxon charter whereby Ethelwolf, King of the West Saxons, granted to the Cathedral twenty manses of land. The latter is signed by the king himself, by his sons, and by St. Swithun, Bishop of Winchester, and is dated 854. A Charter of the new foundation of Winchester Cathedral (with seal attached)—32nd Henry VIII. Sarum Missal, printed by John Higman, at Paris, 1500—a few pages at the end by R. Pynson, London, 1504; Great seal of Henry V; Bishops Gardiner, Fox, and Woodlock's finger rings, with one found in the stone coffin of William Rufus.

MEMORIAL WINDOW TO C. MAYO, Esq., and his son DR. CHARLES MAYO.—(North Aisle). Subjects:—Angel with Censer; Prayers and Praises.—Arms of Bishop.—William of Wykeham's.—St. Swithun, (15th of July, the day of Dr. Mayo's death at Sea).—St. James the Great, (Patron Saint of Avebury, Wilts).—William of Wykeham, (with New College or Cathedral).—St. Cuthberga, (Foundress of Wimborne Minster Architecture).—St. Luke, (the Beloved Physician).—St. Cecilia, (with Organ and Music).

MEMORIAL WINDOW TO COUNTESS OF GUILDFORD.—(North Aisle). SCROLLS:—CONJUGI. *Carissimæ, Dulcissimæ, Sanctissimæ.*—(Most dear, Most sweet, Most holy Wife). FIDES. *Sperandarum Substantia Rerum.*—(*Faith* is the substance of things hoped for.—HEB. xi, 1). CHARITAS. *Patiens est Benigna est.*—(*Charity* suffereth long and is kind.—1 COR. xiii, 4). SPES. *Ad finem firmam retineamus.*—(If we hold fast the confidence and the rejoicing of the *Hope* firm unto the end.—HEB. iii, 6). VERITAS. *Labium firmum erit in perpetuum.*—(The lip of *Truth* shall be established for ever.—PROV. xii, 19). HUMILITAS. *Gloriam præcedit Humilitas.*—(Before Honour is *Humility.*—PROV. xv, 33). PATIENTIA. *Tribulatio Patientiam operatur.*—(Tribulation worketh *Patience.*—ROM. v, 3).

illuminated copy recently prepared at Winchester for the use of the Refectory, he begged it from the Prior, and sent it to Witham, without a hint as to where he got it. The brotherhood were enchanted with the royal gift, and the more so because the manuscript, magnificent as it was, had still room for some additions of their own work in illumination and ornament. The chance visit, however, of a Winchester monk soon disclosed the king's meanness, and the grief which his brethren felt at the loss of a treasure on which they had spent immense pains. Hugh resolved at once to restore the book, though, at the request of the Winchester monks, he did so without the knowledge of the king, and it remains here to this day as a monument of his high principle. This incident seems to have commenced a close friendship between the societies of Witham and St. Swithun.

A.D. 1563.—CHAPTER HOUSE—(at end of South Transept)—and various buildings of the Priory, destroyed by Bishop Horne.

Bishop Horne (1561) distinguished by his controversial writings, appears to have entertained a great aversion to images, etc., erected in churches, and removed the crucifixes and such other paintings and images as were deemed obnoxious to the dominant party. He also destroyed the numerous statues and chapels which adorned the Cathedral, together with the chapter-house and cloisters on the south side of the building.

EARLY WORK (PORTIONS WHICH REMAIN).

A.D. 1079—93.—THE EARLY NORMAN CATHEDRAL. Bishop Walkelin (a relation of William the Conqueror) rebuilt the Cathedral from the West Front to the great Tower, including the Transepts. ST. SWITHUN'S golden shrine was removed with great pomp from the old altar to that erected by Bishop Walkelin.

As the work of rebuilding advanced, Bishop Walkelin found himself distressed by the want of timber. He applied to William the Conqueror for a grant—which without much reflection was made—of as much wood as he could fell and carry away from the wood of Hanepinges, (on the road to Alresford,) in three days. Walkelin collected together all the woodmen of the country, and cut down and carted every tree in the forest in the prescribed time. The king, returning to Winchester a few days after, looked about for the wood, saying that his eyes were either fascinated, or that he had lost his senses, as he could not discover the forest which existed there a short time before. His attendants, however, explained the circumstance, which at first irritated his majesty against the bishop, the king remarking:—'Most assuredly, Walkelyn, I was too liberal, you too exacting in the use made of it.'

A.D. 1107.—GREAT TOWER fell October 7th, and its rebuilding was soon after commenced.

The former Tower of Ely Cathedral was built by Simeon, a brother of Walkelin, the builder of the first Norman tower at Winchester. As generally known both towers proved insecure—Walkelin's Tower at Winchester fell A.D. 1107, and Simeon's Tower at Ely fell A.D. 1321. The fall of the Winchester tower was at the time regarded as a judgment for burying in a sacred precinct so profane a person as William Rufus.

THE PRESENT BELLS.—Three of these bear date 1734; one 1737, one 1742, one 1772, one 1804, and one 1814.

It is recorded that in 1035 Canute gave two bells to the Cathedral; but the oldest bell in Winchester is at St. John's Church, of date 1571.*

EARLY HISTORY.

A.D.

169.—FIRST CHURCH. Christianity was early taught here by preachers from Rome, and the first Church is said to have been built by KING LUCIUS in the form of a cross, with Monastery attached.

Lucius was a lineal descendant of a valiant British chief, whom the Romans named Caractacus.

266.—This Church was destroyed, and Clergy martyred, during the persecution of the Christians by the Emperor Diocletian.

293.—A SECOND CHURCH was erected and Christian worship restored during the reign of the Emperor Constantine, whose son Constans was for a time a monk in the Monastery attached to this Cathedral.

515.—CERDIC, founder of the Kingdom of Wessex, slaughtered the Clergy, and converted this Church into a 'Temple of Dagon,' in which he was crowned A.D. 519, and buried A.D. 534.

635.—CHURCH BUILT THIRD TIME.—KYNEGILS, Cerdic's great grandson, on his conversion by St. Birinus, the first of Saxon bishops, removed the then existing buildings, and commenced a third Church, which his son KYNEWALCH completed A.D. 648.

Kynegils granted the whole of the land around the City for the space of seven miles for the support of the monks of the Monastery attached to this Cathedral.

* See Pamphlet on *Church Bells*, by Rev. A. Du Boulay Hill.

A.D.
852—860.—Kynewalch's buildings were enlarged and repaired by ST. SWITHUN.

Swithun, Bishop of Winchester, Tutor to King Alfred and St. Ethelwold, besides being honoured as the weather saint of the English calendar, is regarded as the special patron of this City. William of Malmesbury speaks of him as being a 'treasury of virtue.' St. Swithun established a scriptorium in the Monastery attached to the Cathedral Church at Winchester, and in it many beautifully illuminated books were, in after years, produced; one example—the Benedictional of St. Ethelwold, now in the possession of the Duke of Devonshire.

St. Swithun, by his own desire, was buried *outside* the north door of the Nave, near the west front. The removal of his body to the inside of the Church was delayed for forty days by continual rain: hence the rhyme:—

'St. Swithun's day, if thou dost rain,
For forty days it will remain;
St. Swithun's day, if thou be faire,
For forty days 'twill raine nae maire.'

Gay writes:—

'If on St. Swithun's feast the welkin lowers,
And every pent-house streams with hasty showers;
Twice twenty days shall clouds their fleeces drain,
And wash the pavement with incessant rain.'

Rudborne states that St. Swithun performed no miracles while the secular Canons inhabited the Church of Winchester, but the moment they were ejected by St. Ethelwold, the miracles began.

In the Benedictional of St. Ethelwold, there is a representation of a belfry consisting of three stories; the roof ends in a point, from which springs a long upright rod, crowned with a vane. This probably belonged to his Cathedral (Winchester), which he rebuilt; the work being completed by his successor, St. Uphege, who, in the place of belfry, added a five-storied tower. Anglo-Saxon architects, with a view to ornament as well as utility, generally removed the tower from its former position outside buildings, and raised it of stone over the middle of the transept in cruciform churches, supporting it on four pillars, formed together by arches.

871.—The third Church also reduced to an almost ruinous state during an attack upon the City by the Danes.

885.—Portions of the Cathedral restored by ALFRED THE GREAT.

980.—Monastery rebuilt by St. Ethelwold, Bishop of Winchester; water introduced, Church extensively repaired, and many Chapels added. These works were completed and added to by St. Uphege.

A.D. 980, St. Ethelwold removed from their first resting-place the remains of ST. SWITHUN, and placed them in a golden shrine.

THE CRYPTS, strikingly suggestive of their great antiquity, and which by many are regarded as portions of St. Ethelwold's work, shew that the original [Saxon ?] Cathedral was terminated at the east end by a circular apse. All the kings of Wessex, and many kings, princes, and bishops of Saxon, Norman, and later times, were buried in these crypts. During the repair of the fabric, commenced in 1818, several feet of earth were placed in the crypts.

Existing Cathedral occupied nearly four centuries in building—from the Conquest to the Reformation.

MODERN WORK.

A.D.

1818.—RESTORATIONS—Tenth pier, South Aisle, (from West) of Nave rebuilt; Bishop's Throne erected; new wooden ceilings to Transepts; Chantries restored, etc., at a cost of £40,000.

1856.—THE ORGAN (by *Willis*) erected.—It was in the Exhibition of 1851.

1860.—WEST FRONT restored at a cost of £3000.

1876.—CHOIR SCREEN (by Sir G. Scott) erected as a memorial of BISHOP WILBERFORCE and DEAN GARNIER.

—— LADY CHAPEL REREDOS, erected by DEAN BRAMSTON.

—— The whole length of the Nave made available for Evening Services by gas-jets arranged on the piers.

1877.—The eleven PINNACLES on the North Aisle restored.

—— NEW LEAD ROOF on South Transept.

1878.—Monument to BISHOP WILBERFORCE erected.

1879-81.—Repairs to mullions of most of the windows, to external arcading of De Lucy's work, and releading many windows, etc.

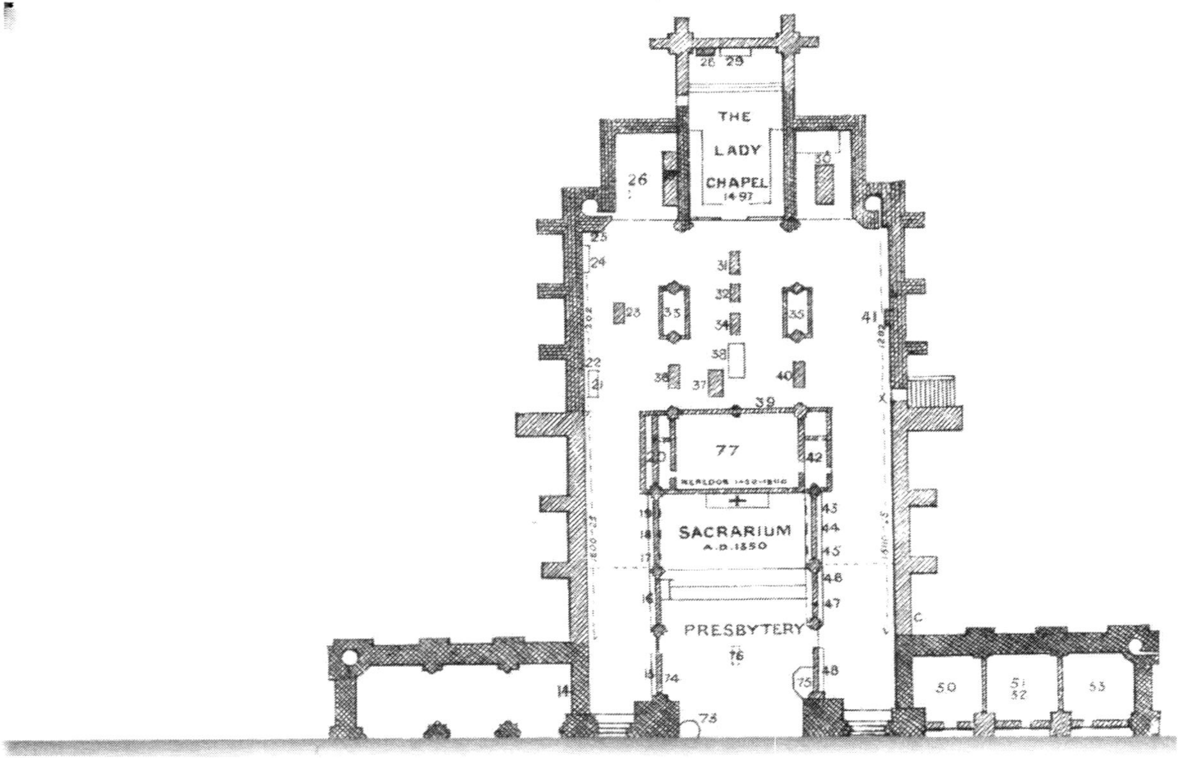
THE
LADY
CHAPEL
1497
SACRARIUM
A.D. 1350
PRESBYTERY
77

References to Figures on Ground Plan.

To those numbers marked with * Inscriptions in full, etc., are given in the text.

(M) Refers to the Mortuary Chests placed near the High Altar by Bishop Henry de Blois in 1129—1171, and by Bishop Fox in 1524.

1. Vestibule. Tribune or Gallery for minstrels, over.
2.* Monument of the two Brothers of Avington, placed over No. 3.
3.* Monumental brass in Memory of Jane Austen, authoress.
4.* Mrs. Montagu (1800), Founder of the Blue Stocking Club, and Chimney Sweepers' Friend.
5.* Early Norman Font.
O* Anonymous.
6. Floor Slab Monument to Dean Kingsmill (last Benedictine Prior and first Dean, died A.D. 1548).
7. Bishop Walkelin (1098).
8.* Colonel Boles, Royalist (1641). Small brass on pillar.
9. Bishop Morley's Tomb (1684). Founder of Widows' College.
10. Bishop Hoadley (1761).
11. Choristers' Practice Room.
12. Prebendary Iremonger's Tomb, by *Chantrey* (1820).
13.* Chapel of Holy Sepulchre.
14. Modern entrance to Crypt.
15. (M) Canute, Rufus, Queen Emma, and Bishops Wina and Alwin, also miscellaneous bones.
16. (M) Kenulph, 714, and Egbert, 837.
17. Bishop I de Pontissara (1304), Founder of St. Elizabeth's College.
18. (M) Kynegils, 641, Adulphus (Ethelwolf), 857.
19.* Hardicanute (1042).
20.* Bishop Gardiner's Chantry (1555.)
21. Unknown.
22.* Wm. Symonds (1616), Founder of Christ's Hospital.
23.* Bishop Peter de Rupibus (1238).
24. Thomas Mason.
25.* The heart of Bishop Ethelmar.
26.* Chapel of Guardian Angels. (Bishop Orlton's Chantry.)
27. R. Weston, Cavalier (1634).
28. Bishop Brownlow North, by *Chantrey* (1820).
29. Lady Chapel Reredos, erected by Dean Bramston, 1876.
30.* Bishop de Langton's Chantry.
31. Bishop Godfrey de Lucy, (1204), Buried in the midst of his own work.
32.* Wm. Rufus' Tomb (1100), Removed from Presbytery.
33.* Bishop Waynflete's Chantry (1486).
34. Sir Arnald de Gavaston (1302), The only ancient military effigy in the Cathedral.
35.* Cardinal Beaufort's Chantry (1447).
36. Unknown.
37. Bishop Sumner (1874).
38.* Prior Silkstede (1524).
39.* Entrance to Crypts, called the 'Holy Hole,' closed by Bishop Fox (1518).
40.* Prior William de Basynge (1295).
41. Sir John Cloberly (1680), Supporter of Charles II.
42.* Bishop Fox's Chantry (1520).
43. Richard, younger son of William the Conqueror.
44. (M) Edred (955).
45. Edward, eldest son of Alfred the Great, in Saxon (924). [(946).
46. (M) Edmund, son of Alfred, murdered,
47. Heart of Bishop N. de Ely (1280). Body buried at Waverley.
48. (M) Miscellaneous bones of Princes, collected 1644
49. Sir Isaac Townsend (1731).
50.* Venerable Chapel.
51.* Prior Silkstede's Chapel.
52.* Izaak Walton, 'Prince of Fishermen.'
53.* Ancient Calefactory.
54.* Entrance Lobby.
55.* Ancient Staircase.
56. Memorial to Officers and Men of the 7th Royal Fusiliers who died during the Crimean War, 1854-5.
57. The Treasury or Sacristy.
58. Memorial to Officers and Men of the 101st Regiment who died in action or from wounds received at Umballa Pass, 20th Oct. to 25th Dec. 1863.
59. Sir J. Campbell. 18th June, 1855.
60. Sir G. Prevost, by *Chantrey* (1816).
61.* Bishop Edyngton's Chantry (1366).
62. General Knollys (1818).
63. Dean Naylor (1739).
64.* Bishop Willis, by *Cheere* (1743).
65.* William of Wykeham's Chantry, [(1404).
66. Dean Cheney (1760).
67. Bishop Tomline, by *R. Westmacott, jun.* (1827).
68. Dr. Warton, by *Flaxman* (1800).
69. Henrietta Maria North, by *Flaxman* (1796).
70. 71. Monumental Tablets in Memory of Officers and Men Killed at the Siege of Sevastopol in 1854-5. The old regimental colours are suspended near.
72. Lecterne.
73. Pulpit, by Prior Silkstede (1520). Canopy later.
74. Bishop Toclyve (1189), Founder of Hospital, St. Mary Magdalene.
75. Bishop's Throne.
76. Spot where tomb of Rufus was.
77.* Feretory.

Canute the Great (1035) and Bishop Henry de Blois (1171) were buried before the High Altar.

A Figure of James I, in bronze.

B Figure of Charles I, in bronze.

ENVIRONS OF THE CATHEDRAL.

The total area of the Cathedral and its precincts, including Wolvesey, is thirty-five acres. On the north side of the present churchyard formerly stood the NEWAN MYNSTRE, afterwards removed, in the year 1110, to the north of the City, and called 'Hyde Abbey.' On a portion of its site now stands a College endowed by Bishop Morley, and providing a separate dwelling-house each for ten clergymen's widows. On the site of the adjoining approach to the churchyard, called the Square, stood the older Royal Castle, which was standing at the time of the Conquest. This Palace made the approach to the Cathedral less direct, and was therefore entirely taken down by Bishop de Blois (1129-1171). The signs of a round mass of flint masonry, on the south-west of the Cathedral front, indicate the fortifications which protected the precinct from the incursions of the Danes, and, during the reign of Henry III, from a tumultuous populace. In the south wall, near the west front, are the fragments of a doorway supposed to be portions of the 'chapel, with a carnary,' or bone-house, mentioned by Leland. The Cathedral Nave and South Aisle being used as a thoroughfare to the Close, the passage called 'the Slype' was opened, by cutting through the great buttress on the south side, commemorated, (on the west side of the opening,) by the following anagram :—

☜ ILL   PREC
\   \
AC   ATOR
/   /
H   VI ☞
AMBULA

ILLAC PRECATOR, HAC VIATOR AMBULA.

That way thou who comest to pray, this way thou who art pursuing thy journey, walk.

The anagram over an arch on the east side :—

1632.

CESSIT COMMUNI PROPRIUM, JAM PURGITE QUA FAS.

Private property has yielded to public utility. Proceed now by the way which is open to thee.

And :—

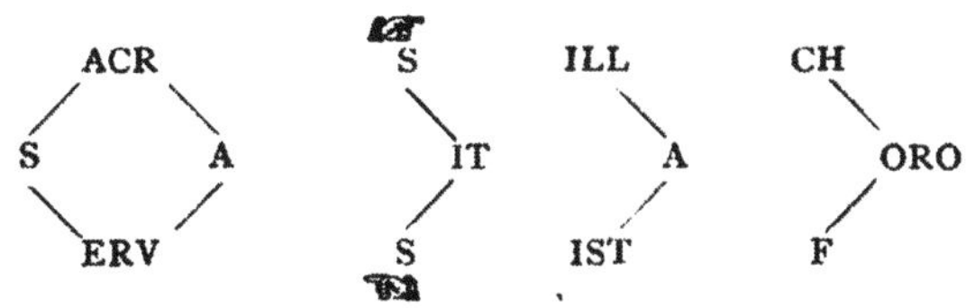

SACRA SIT ILLA CHORO, SERVA SIT ISTA FORO.

That way is consecrated to the choir, this way leads to the market.

Near this Slype was a doorway or turning which communicated with the cellarer's offices, where, after long vigils, the monks, with the permission of a superior, could call for a cup of beer.

Passing through the Slype we enter upon the site of the ancient Cloisters and Chapter-house.* The five Early Norman entrance arches to the latter remain, and the internal arcading may still be traced in a series of small arches south of the South Transept. In this Chapter-house Archbishop Langton absolved King John from interdict, proceeding afterwards to the choir to celebrate the Holy Communion, which had been suspended for six years.

Vestiges of an old Conventual Dormitory are to be seen in the angle of what once was an extension of the south wall of the Chapter-house—namely, a narrow oblique window, and a little further on the trace of a stone staircase; also the base of an Early English column, and the substructure of the huge *necessarium*, consisting of fifteen arches over the old branch of the Lock Pond, and part of a second row parallel to it. Nearer to the Deanery is an Early English doorway with bold mouldings and shafts of Purbeck marble. It lead to the Dormitory and Infirmary.

The entrance to the Deanery (temp. Hen. III) consists of three acute arches, forming the vestibule, all of which were open

* Chapter-house taken down 1570 for the sake of the lead on its roof.

at one time, and were probably connected with the Cloisters. Some narrow lancet niches, above the arches, should be noticed. The Prior's Hall (15th century) has a fine roof and windows, but has long been divided into apartments.

Charles II occasionally lodged at the Deanery during the time Sir Christopher Wren was building his palace. About this time Bishop Ken, then a Prebendary of the Cathedral, refused to let Nell Gwyne have his house. On the Bishopric of Bath and Wells becoming vacant, Charles II showed that he bore no ill-will by appointing Ken to the See,—inquiring, 'Where is the good little man who refused his lodging to poor Nell?' A small building was put up for her on the south of the Deanery, which was pulled down early in the present century. A house in Colebrook Street, outside the precinct, was also occupied by Nelly.

In the Dean's stable, a wooden building (formerly the Strangers' Hall), may be seen a wooden roof, constructed about 1280. Parker says, 'the work is of rude character, more like a good barn roof than that of a hall.'

In the basement of a house, on the west of the Close, are some finely vaulted apartments, said to have been part of the kitchen and buttery of the Monastery.

The wooden doors of the old gateway, leading out of the Close, towards the Kingsgate, probably date from the thirteenth century. The gates were burnt in 1264 in the rising of the citizens against the Prior and Convent of St. Swithun. The Druidical stones near this gateway will be noted with interest.

Near this Close gateway is the old Cheyney Court, or the Court-house of the episcopal jurisdiction of the Soke of Winchester. Considerable business was formerly transacted in Cheyney Court, but the city police take from it the criminal business which made the prison in St. John Street a necessary adjunct. Only manorial business is now done in connection with this court. No explanation of its name has been found. The old barge-boards of this and the adjoining house, and the internal arrangements of the Court are worth notice.

Winchester Cathedral from the South East,
shewing Saxon Arches, and portion of Chapter Room Arcading

Winchester College.

For a Conductor apply at the Porter's Lodge in the Gateway.]

Founding of the College.

SEINTE MARIE COLLEGE OF WYNCHESTRE, the parent of Eton, and the model of Westminster, was founded March 26th, A.D. 1387, by Bp. William of Wykeham.

Near the same spot, long before the Norman Conquest, there had been a grammar school. Rudborne, in his history,* states that King Ethelwolf and King Alfred were educated at this School; and Bp. Henry de Blois† (1129—1171), in his statutes relating to St. Cross Hospital, also refers to certain of the scholars.

Bp. William of Wykeham himself had been educated at this earlier School, and it is probable that it had afterwards fallen into decay. Thus its re-establishment, on an enlarged basis, suggested itself to Bp. Wykeham's mind.

The foundation of Winchester College, under the governance of a powerful corporation, allied to one of the principal Colleges at Oxford, was a marked advance on the old system, which had left the early training of Scholars generally in the hands of monks belonging to the local monasteries.

* Pp. 199; 207. † *Chron. Monast. de Abingdon*, vol. ii, p. 255.

THE COLLEGE BUILDINGS.

During the building of the College, Bp. Wykeham removed the scholars to temporary houses on St. Giles' Hill. The new buildings occupied six years in their erection, and were entered in procession on the 28th March, 1393,* headed by :—

	Representing
John Morys, the Warden, and others representing ten Fellows†	The Eleven Apostles (Judas omitted).
The Head Master, Second Master, and Seventy Scholars	The Seventy-two Disciples (Vulgate number).
Three Chaplains and three Clerks ..	The Six faithful Deacons (Nicholas apostatised).
Sixteen Choristers	Four great and twelve minor Prophets.

The early College buildings form two quadrangles.‡ In the forecourt is the Second Master's residence; and, as in other ancient foundations, the brewhouse and Warden's stables are placed here, together with a bakehouse, malt and flourhouse, and a butcher's house§ now pulled down. The front of the buildings in College Street (nearly 300 feet, exclusive of the Head Master's residence) is in strict character with their less importance, and of strength sufficient to have served as a defence in troublous times. The best view of the College buildings is from the south side.

THE OUTER GATEWAY is massive, and in the central niche, facing College Street, is an ancient statue of the Virgin Mary. Over the groining of this gateway is the Bursary. The statues over the gateway to the middle court represent the Virgin Mary, the Angel Gabriel, and the Founder; the barbaric heads on the surrounding corbels serve as contrasts to these.

* Three years previous to the founding of Winchester College, Wykeham had commenced his College at Oxford.

† The first nomination of Fellows, five in number, took place in 1394. The remaining five were probably nominated a year later. They could not therefore have taken place in the procession in 1393.

‡ The Commoners reside in nine large Tutors' Houses, which are adjacent.

§ The Warden's house occupies the site of these.

IN THE INNER QUADRANGLE the whole of the principal offices form one length of about 100 feet. The grotesque carvings above the windows severally refer to the uses of the apartments. On the hall and kitchen entrance are the psaltery and bagpipe; over kitchen window, Excess, a head vomiting; opposite a Bursar as Frugality, with his iron bound money-chest; over the Masters' windows are the Pedagogue, the Listless Scholar, etc. Some of the sleeping chambers on the basement are now used for 'books.' At the Conduit, on the west side, the Scholars formerly washed under an open porch in all seasons.

THE CHAPEL (93 feet in length, 30 feet in breadth, and 57 feet in height), entered by a vestibule,* leading to the Cloisters, deserves careful notice. It is lightened by lofty and elegant Perpendicular windows, filled with rich stained glass, and outside imposing buttresses intervene each window. The grand Eastern window, the subject of a poem by Bp. Lowth, portrays the genealogy of our Saviour. In the centre is a representation of the Crucifixion, and in the highest panel, of St. Peter, St. Paul, and the Resurrection. Small figures of Simon

* This vestibule has been decorated by *Butterfield*, in memory of the thirteen Wykehamists who fell in the Crimean war. Elsewhere we give the inscriptions in full.

Membury, clerk of the works, William Wynford, the mason, with the carpenter and glazier, are shown at the head and feet of Jesse. Mr. Winston states that all this glass, with the exception of half-a-dozen small pieces, is modern (1824) and pronounces the Jesse window to be 'a very good *copy* of the old design.'

The graceful fan tracery ceiling in wood (an invention of Wykeham's) has been preserved entire, but for the original reredos and carved stalls, Grecian work was substituted. The new reredos was the gift of Chief Justice Earle, and more appropriate fittings take the place of the Grecian furniture. The screen, which used to form an Ante-chapel has been removed, and there is now only the Chapel and the Chantry of Warden Thurburn, built 1470, rebuilt with the Tower 1863. The present Organ was rebuilt and enlarged by *Bishop & Son*, in 1875.

The restoration of the REREDOS was completed in 1877, by the placing in position the twelve statues representing SS. Peter, John the Divine, Stephen, Augustine of Hippo, Benedict, Paul, James, Alban, Augustine of Canterbury, and Boniface, the latter being the Bishop who went from Nursling to evangelize the Germans. On the right is commemorated the tradition that Alfred the Great was educated (by St. Swithun) near the present foundation, and, with pious reverence to the founder, William of Wykeham finds a place on the left. The work was executed by Eardley, of Westminster.

In 1470, the TOWER, with turret and pinnacles, was built with money left by Warden Thurburn, which (owing to the giving way of the foundation) was rebuilt in 1863, and called the 'Tower of the Two Wardens,' in memory of Robert Speckott Barter, Warden of Winchester, and David Williams, Warden of New College. Most of the old stones were replaced in their original positions. In this tower is a good-toned peal of six bells, some of which are of ancient date.

THE SACRISTY is on the north-east of the Chapel. It was originally furnished with a tabernacle of gold with chalice and phials of the same metal, the gift of Henry VI. Above the Sacristy is the MUNIMENT ROOM. The original window shutters are cased in iron, and the old chests contain the ancient deeds and charters of the College. Note the travelling cases for the mitre of Wm. of Wykeham; the worm-eaten lockers for the copes, and the curious drawers in which the title deeds and bulls were placed; all in *statu quo* as in the fourteenth century.

Many of the monumental brasses, which originally enriched Chapel pavement, have been removed to Cloisters.

THE CLOISTERS (Perpendicular) retain their uniqueness and quiet. The length of each side of the square is 132 feet. The rafters are of chestnut (or Irish oak) which is said to account for the absence of every species of worm and cobweb. The roofing is covered in with Somersetshire stone tiles of great durability as well as weight. For more than four centuries the Cloisters have been the burial place of those associated with the College. Among the ancient epitaphs is the following:—

'Edmund Hodson, Clerk, and Fellow of this College,
died the 8th of August, 1580.
Who so thou art, with loving harte,
Stande, read, and thinke on me,
For as I was, so now thou art,
And as I am, so shalt thou be.'

The plain part of the stonework bears many incised names of former scholars—'Thos. Ken, 1646'; 'Francis Turner, 1655'; 'Thomas Warton,' etc. Ken's Evening and Morning Hymns first appeared in a Manual of Prayers written by him for the use of Winchester Scholars. His organ was preserved many years over 'third chamber.'

The CHANTRY CHAPEL, with Scriptorium above it, situate in the square of the Cloisters, was built by John Fromond, the

Founder's steward, at whose cost the Cloisters also were built about 1430. The glass in the East window (date 1470) was removed from Thurburn's chantry. The roof is richly groined. It was suppressed as a chantry by Henry VIII. After being used for nearly two centuries as the Library, it is now fitted as a chapel for Junior Scholars. The Library is placed in the Scriptorium above.

THE REFECTORY OR HALL is 63 feet long by 30 feet wide. It has a finely groined oak roof; its centre elevated and perforated for ventilation. At the upper end is a daïs where, on particular occasions, sit the Warden and Fellows; and on which the Wykehamical grace is usually sung by the Scholars after dinner. At the lower end are the butteries, from which provisions are dispensed. Near these stands the 'tub' for broken victuals for the poor; formerly there was a Prefect of Tub. Ale was poured from old 'leathern jacks,' and the square wooden trenchers, which formerly served as plates, are now used for bread only. Above the butteries is the ancient Audit Room, with timber roof, paved with Flemish tiles, and partly hung with fifteenth century tapestries (representing the story of David and Nabal, etc.); and the coats of mail formerly worn by the Warden's escort (or 'plump of spears'). Here also is the Founder's iron-bound treasure-chest, secured by three locks, and a functior (candlestick), used in all the chambers. In the small Library in the roof above, the College account books were kept; the door and lock should be noticed. The Cellar has a vaulted ceiling supported by a central pillar, and a groined staircase direct from the Hall.

THE KITCHEN is lofty, and has no apartment over it. In it, on the visitation of the Bishop, in 1410, a pair of porpoises were cooked.

PAINTING OF THE TRUSTY SERVANT.

In the passage is the curious picture of 'The Trusty Servant.' The original painting was most probably made in the sixteenth century, but since then it has been more than once repainted. The present picture is of the time of Queen Anne. The words are attributed to Dr. C. Johnson (Head Master, 1560—71).

Effigiem servi si vis spectare probati,
Quisquis es, hæc oculos pascat imago tuos;
Porcinum os quocunque cibo jejunia sedat;
Hæc sera, consilium ne fluat, arcta premit;
Dat patientem asinus dominis jurgantibus aurem;
Cervus habet celeres ire, redire, pedes;
Læva docet multum tot rebus onusta laborem;
Vestis munditiem; dextera aperta fidem;
Accinctus gladio; clypeo munitus; et inde
Vel se, vel dominum, quo tueatur habet.

A trusty servant's portrait would you see,
This emblematic figure well survey;
The porker's snout—not nice in diet shows;
The padlock shut—no secrets he'll disclose;
Patient the ass—his master's wrath to bear;
Swiftness in errand—the stag's feet declare;
Loaded his left hand—apt to labour saith;
The vest—his neatness; open hand—his faith;
Girt with his sword—his shield upon his arm—
Himself and master he'll protect from harm.

ROYAL VISITS.—The College roll of royal patrons and visitors is a long one. We extract the following :—

Henry VI (the founder of Eton) was a frequent attendant at the Chapel Services ;

Edward IV, on the 20th January, 1471, mindful of boys' pleasures, sent the Scholars a lion to look at ;

Henry VII, on the birth of Prince Arthur at Winchester, visited the College ;

Henry VIII paid his second visit, in company with the Emperor Charles V ;

In July, 1553, a mighty stir without the College Gates announced the arrival of Queen Mary and her Consort, Philip of Spain ;*

In the *Computus* is the following reference to an entertainment on this occasion :—

1553. For 16 tuns of double beer when the king and queen came to the college, 0:16:4; cloves by the lb. 0:5:4; mace, 0:16:0; cinnamon, 0:5:4; pepper, 0:2:6; currants, 0:0:5½.

Queen Mary and her Consort made offerings in the chapel :—

A.D. 1553, 25 Julii.

The kinges almes . . .	x*li.*	xvi*s.*	viij*d.*
The quenes almes . . .	vj*li.*	xiiij*s.*	iiij*d.*
My lorde of Chychester . .		xx*s.*	
Summa . . .	xviij*li.*	x*s.*	

Queen Elizabeth visited the College, when orations and verses were recited before her by forty of the Scholars.

In 1547 three Royal Commissioners—Hales, Cave, and Bridges—visited the College. The first injunction from them was :—'That from henceforth the Bible shall be daily read in English distinctly and apertly in the midst of the hall, above the hearth, where the fire is made, both at dinner and supper.'

In November, 1603, King James I, sent a sudden summons to the Warden, requesting the society to quit their chambers, and allow the judges, the sheriffs, and chief lawyers of the realm, to lodge in them, while they held their court in the Great Hall of Winchester Castle for the trial of Sir Walter Raleigh, who was there condemned to death for high treason against James I, but subsequently reprieved. After his release from prison, he sailed for the coast of Guiana, with fifteen armed

* See Walcott's *William of Wykeham and his Colleges*.

ships, on an unsuccessful search for gold. On his return, in 1616, the king, partly to please the Spaniards, ordered his execution.

THE SCHOOLROOM.—The 'old' Schoolroom was under the Hall, and was afterwards converted into a Dormitory and called 'Seventh Chamber.' This Schoolroom was built by Warden Nicholas in 1687. Over the entrance is a bronze statue of Wykeham, cast by *Cibber*. Cibber's eldest son, on presentation as Founder's kin by his mother, was rejected; but when the younger son, Lewis, presented himself, the artist (to make this boy's election the more certain) presented a statue of the Founder, 'whereupon,' writes Colley, 'the door of preferment was opened.' The Schoolroom is now used for meetings of the Glee Club, etc.

On the western wall are inscriptions with emblems:—

* AUT DISCE. A mitre and crozier, as the expected rewards of learning.

† AUT DISCEDE. An inkhorn and sword, the emblems of the civil and military professions.

‡ MANET SORS TERTIA CÆDI. A scourge.

At the east end are placed the following rules for the conduct of the students, written in Latin, in the style of the famous *Duodecim Tabulæ* of the Romans.

TABLE OF THE SCHOLASTIC LAWS.

IN THE CHURCH.—Worship God. Say your prayers with a pious affection of the mind. Let not your eyes wander about. Keep silence. Read nothing profane.

IN THE SCHOOL.—Let each one be diligent in his studies. Let him repeat his lesson in a low tone of voice to himself, but in a clear tone to his master. Let no one give disturbance to his neighbour. Take care to spell your theme aright. Have all your school implements in constant readiness.

IN THE HALL.—Whoever says grace, let him repeat it distinctly. The rest are all to answer him. All are in the meantime to stand upright in their places. Whatever is to be repeated, let it be clearly and properly pronounced. Whilst you sit at table, behave with due decorum.

IN THE COURT.—Let no one throw stones or balls against the windows. Let not the building be defaced with writing or carving upon it. Let no one approach the masters with his head uncovered, or without a companion.

* Either learn. † Or depart hence. ‡ Or remain and be chastised.

In the Chambers.—Let cleanliness be attended to. Let each one study in the evening, and let silence prevail in the night.

In the Town, going to the Hill.—Let the scholars walk in pairs. Let them behave with proper modesty. Let them move their hats to their masters and other respectable persons. Let decency regulate your countenance, your motions, and your gait. Let no one on the hill go beyond the prescribed limits.

Everywhere and at all Times.—Let the inferiors be subject to the præfects. Let the præfects govern with equity. Let the latter be themselves free from fault, and give good examples to the rest. Let both inferiors and præfects refrain from everything that is unbecoming, both in actions and in words.

Whoever disobeys these rules will be sentenced to condign punishment.

No one will be excused in staying at home beyond the time of the vacation. Those who are detected in going out of the College without leave, will be expelled for the third offence.

Scholarships, etc.

'Besides the College scholarships, there are eight exhibitions of £50 a year tenable by Commoners at Winchester, two of which are usually open to competition at the same examination as the scholarships, and it is further intended to give a certain number of exhibitions in College, relieving those who obtain them from all school expenses. The College also annually grants exhibitions of various amounts to several of those who have acquitted themselves best on their going to the University, in addition to any scholarships they may obtain. These are the leading applications of its endowments............Winchester still remains chiefly a classical school, but not in the whole exclusiveness. Studies other than that of the classics have greatly increased of late years. Either French or German forms part of the regular work in every part of the school. The study of mathematics also has made great progress, and has become a very important part of the teaching. Neither can any boy pass through the school without receiving some instruction in the rudiments of physical science; in short, Winchester offers an education mainly classical, but including, perhaps, as wide a variety of other subjects as can well be got into the twenty-four hours. In the higher departments a boy has considerable opportunities for concentrating his attention more on some of these subjects than others; more especially in the case of mathematics............The natural crown of public school education is to be found at the University, and there it may fairly be claimed that Winchester holds her own.'

The following is the Thanksgiving for the Founder, as at present used on Commemoration days:—

'O, ETERNAL GOD, the Life and the Resurrection of all that believe in Thee, always to be praised as well for the Dead as for those that be Alive, we give Thee most hearty Thanks for our FOUNDER, WILLIAM OF WYKEHAM; and all our other Benefactors, by whose Benefits we are here brought up to Godliness and the studies of good Learning; beseeching Thee that we, well using all these Thy Blessings to the Praise and Honour of Thy Holy Name, may at length be brought to the Immortal Glory of the Resurrection, through Jesus Christ our Lord. *Amen.*'

THE COLLEGE PROPERTY.

In 1545, by the Statute of 37th Henry VIII, sec. 4, the existence of the College was endangered; but an Order in Council, passed in 1547, specially exempted it, together with Eton and the Colleges at Oxford and Cambridge, from the forfeiture of property.

The revenues of the College, in the time of Henry VIII, amounted to £710. In the year 1854 the income amounted to about £15,000.

During the period of the Great Rebellion, Colonel Nathaniel Fiennes (a Fellow of New College, Oxford, and one of the Founder's kin) placed a guard at the College gateway, and thus saved the buildings from the wanton damage committed in the Cathedral by some of Waller's horse soldiers.

A Carmelite Friary occupied the site of the Gymnasium; stone and marble coffins were recently found here.

There was exhibited, during the visit of the Newbury Field Club, in May, 1876, 'on a table in the Warden's gallery, a glazed box containing some interesting parchments, but the Warden explained that there were few of Wykeham's relics kept in Winchester, the great bulk of them being in the custody of the Warden of New College, at Oxford. A plain gold ring, with a large sapphire, which belonged to William of Wykeham, was, however, amongst the articles exhibited here, and some ancient documents, the most ancient bearing date 1382. It was a charter of Richard II, licensing the prior of St. Swithun's of that date to alienate certain lands to found the College. Another exceedingly curious MS. refers to the murder of Thomas à Becket, presented by the Founder himself to the College, and which tradition affirmed had never been allowed to be taken outside its walls. There was likewise a representation, in fancy needlework, of the "Last Supper," of the date of the 15th century; a specimen of the art of Caxton in *The Life of St. Catherine;* an early translation of the Testament in the time of Wycliffe; a work with the title of "Accidence" by Wynkyn de Worde; a copy of Bishop Ken's resignation of his fellowship of the College, when he became a bishop,' etc.*

In the College Library are also some Anglo-Saxon charters, and charters from the conquest to the reign of Charles II; a roll of the household expenses of Bp. Wm. of Wykeham; Raleigh's 'Briefe description of the Newe Founde Lande of Virginia'; and an MS. Vulgate of the 13th century.

The Warden's gallery contains a series of portraits of the Wardens of the College, and of some others who have been associated with it. The old College plate comprises a very fine specimen of a 'loving cup,' and a curious and very large antique salt cellar.

For five centuries, as a nursery of learning, in close connection with the Universities, has Winchester College maintained a

* *Hampshire Chronicle*, June 3, 1876.

foremost place—'a noble monument to the enlightened and far-seeing liberality of its munificent founder.' The list of eminent men who were here educated possesses much historic and literary interest.

Universal testimony leaves no doubt that 'Wykehamists retain in after life a closer sense of brotherhood, than do men from other public schools.'

At the close of the Summer Term, 'Dulce Domum' is sung. Tradition ascribes the song to a scholar kept at College during vacation. It can be traced back for more than a century.

Dulce Domum.

Concinamus, O sodales;
Eja! quid silemus!
    Nobile canticum!
Dulce melos, domum!
Dulce domum, resonemus!

  Domum, domum, dulce domum!
  Domum, domum, dulce domum!
  Dulce, dulce, dulce domum!
  Dulce domum, resonemus!

Appropinquat ecce felix!
    Hora gaudiorum;
Post grave tedium
Advenit omnium
    Meta petita laborum.

Musa libros mitte, fessa;
    Mitte pensa dura,
Mitte negotium,
Jam datur otium,
    Me mea mittito cura.

Ridet annus, prata rident;
    Nosque rideamus.
Jam repetit domum
Daulius advena:
    Nosque domum repetamus.

Heus! Rogere, fer caballos;
    Eja nunc eamus.
Limen amabile,
Matris et oscula,
    Suaviter et repetamus.

Concinamus ad Penates
Vox et audiatur:
Phosphore! quid jubar,
Segnius emicans,
Gaudia nostra moratur?

[*Translation.*]

Sing a sweet melodious measure,
Waft enchanting lays around;
Home! a theme replete with pleasure!
Home! a grateful theme resound!

Home, sweet home! an ample treasure!
Home! with ev'ry blessing crown'd!
Home! perpetual source of pleasure!
Home! a noble strain, resound!

Lo, the joyful hour advances,
Happy season of delight;
Festal songs, and festal dances,
All our tedious toils requite.

Leave, my weary'd muse, thy learning,
Leave thy task, so hard to bear;
Leave thy labour, ease returning,
Leave my bosom, O my care!

See the year, the meadow smiling,
Let us then a smile display;
Rural sports our pain beguiling,
Rural pastimes call away.

Now the swallow seeks her dwelling,
And no longer loves to roam;
Her example thus impelling,
Let us seek our native home.

Let our men and steeds assemble,
Panting for the wide campaign;
Let the ground beneath us tremble,
While we scour along the plain.

O what raptures, O what blisses!
When we gain the lovely gate;
Mother's arms and mother's kisses,
There our blest arrival wait.

Lend, O Lucifer! thy ray;
Greet our household-gods with singing;
Why should light so slowly springing,
All our promis'd joys delay?

From 'The Gentleman's Magazine,' March, 1796.

Public School Fare Seventy Years Ago.—'An Old Wykehamist,' who says that he is an octogenarian and upwards, writing to the *Times* on the subject of fare in public schools, which has exercised many pens of late, says that he is no '*Laudator temporis acti*' as regards 'the *pabulum mentis vel corporis*' then supplied, and that the youth of the present generation are '*fortunati nimium*' in this respect, though he questions whether they may not be brought up too daintily and delicately. He writes :—

'I will now give you our "bill of fare" for the day. We breakfasted at ten o'clock on bread and butter, very little of the latter, with beer *ad libitum.* At one o'clock there was placed on tables in the hall a small quantity of cold boiled beef, which, I know not why, was seldom, if ever, touched, and also a very small quantity of bread and cheese. We dined at six o'clock on joints of mutton all the year round, except on Sundays, when we had roast beef, and at Easter for six weeks we had veal. The joints were served up whole, a leg for eight, and a shoulder for six boys, who formed six "ends" as they were called, or messes. There was no superintendent in the shape of a master. The senior boy of the "end" had the first cut; which was a very ample one; and the joint was handed down, "fine by degrees," not "beautifully less," when the junior of the "end" was a lucky fellow if he found any meat on the bone. It is a fact that I have been three days without any dinner; for, when our seniors were regaling themselves, the juniors had to go down to their chambers to clean the prefects' candlesticks and put other things in order for the evening. On Wednesdays and Fridays we had baked plum puddings, which were very good. We had no vegetables of any kind until we were prefects, and then we paid for them. The reason assigned was that in the time of William of Wykeham potatoes had not been introduced into England, although the Warden and Fellows did not scruple to avail themselves of this comparatively modern esculent. We had beer again *ad libitum.* We had to provide our own knives and forks, and ate off square flat wooden trenchers. At nine o'clock we had in our chambers a little bread and cheese, and again plenty of beer. Those who could afford it had messes of cocoa or coffee, and other food which exercised their culinary faculties. Under this Spartan regimen the boys were exceedingly healthy. Only one death occurred during the eight years that I was in college, and that was occasioned by a sunstroke. "*Tempora mutantur,*" and no doubt, on the whole, for the better.'

Crimean Monument in the Porch of the Chapel of Winchester College.

FAITH VIRTUE KNOWLEDGE TEMPERANCE PATIENCE CHARITY

Samuel Twyford, R.N.,
Lieutenant H.M.S. 'London,'
Killed in the Trenches
while serving in the
Royal Naval Brigade,
9th April, 1855,
Aged twenty-five years.

Edward Henry Webb,
Lieut. 88th Connaught Rangers
Killed in the Attack on the
Quarries,
7th June, 1855,
Aged twenty-two years.

Frederick Grote Barker,
Lieut. 68th Light Infantry,
Killed at the Battle of Inkerman
5th November, 1854
Aged twenty-one years.

Richard Grenville Deane,
Ensign 30th Regiment of Foot,
Killed at the Assault on the
Redan,
8th September, 1855,
Aged eighteen years.

Walter Trevelyan,
Colonel Coldstream Guards,
Died of Cholera at Varna,
21st August, 1854,
Aged fifty-six years.

Robert Edward Boyle, M.P.,
Son of Edmund Earl of Cork
and Orrery,
Lieut.-Col. Coldstream Guards,
Died of Fever at Varna,
3rd September, 1854,
Aged forty-four years.

Henry Thomas Butler,
Captain 55th Regiment of Foot,
Deputy-Assistant-Adjutant-General,
Killed at the Battle of
Inkerman,
5th November, 1854,
Aged forty-one years.

This Porch
HAS BEEN PREPARED AND
BEAUTIFIED BY
**William of Wykeham's
Sons**
AS A SACRED SHRINE,
IN WHICH THE MEMORIES OF
THEIR THIRTEEN BRETHREN
WHO DIED
IN THE WAR OF THE CRIMEA,
A.D. 1854-5,
MAY BE PRESERVED FOR AN
EXAMPLE TO FUTURE
GENERATIONS.

—

Think upon them thou who art
passing by to-day;
Child of the same family, bought
by the same Lord;
Keep thy foot when thou goest
into this house of God;
There watch thine armour, and
make thyself ready by prayer,
To fight and to die,
The faithful soldier and servant
of Christ and of thy country.

John Jackson Lowth, C.B.,
Lieutenant-Colonel
38th Regiment of Foot,
Died on Landing at Portsmouth
28th July, 1855,
from wounds received on
the 18th June,
Aged fifty-one years.

John Charles Conolly,
Captain
23rd Royal Welsh Fusiliers,
Killed at the battle of the
Alma,
20th September, 1854,
Aged thirty-three years.

Frank John Curtis,
Lieut. 46th Regiment of Foot,
Killed in the Trenches,
2nd May, 1855,
Aged twenty-three years.

Arthur Francis Maine,
Lieut, 77th Regiment of Foot,
Died in Camp,
21st November, 1854,
Aged twenty-two years.

James Bullen Dennis,
Lieutenant 3rd Buffs,
Died 4th October, 1855,
of wounds received in the
Trenches before Sebastopol,
19th August, 1855,
Aged twenty-one years.

Charles Henry Beck,
Lieutenant
23rd Royal Welsh Fusiliers,
Died at Sea,
29th September, 1855,
of wounds received at the
Assault on the Redan,
Aged nineteen years.

He ∴ is ∴ not ∴ a ∴ God ∴ of ∴ the ∴ Dead ∴ but ∴ of ∴ the ∴ Living, ∴ for ∴ all ∴ live ∴ unto ∴ Him.

S. Cross.—Beaufort's Tower.—A. D. 1440.

EXTERIOR OF PORTER'S LODGE.

The Ancient Hospital of St. Cross.

[One mile from Winchester on the Southampton road.]

WHAT better site on which to dedicate
A noble tribute of undying love
To that Great Cross, the Source of all our hope,
The Fount of grace and tender charity?

See how the light comes flickering through the trees,
Throwing weird shadows on the dewy sward,
Where all around the peaceful cattle graze;
While close beside the walls a streamlet flows,
Which meets ere long the Itchen's rolling tide,
And gently merges there its separate course.

In this fair spot, where Nature is unchecked,
And all the works of God are manifest,
Scarce tainted by the spoiling hand of man,
How many a life has found a blissful close! ACANTHUS.*

THERE is no Institution existing at the present time in Great Britain, which has been suffered to remain, for upwards of seven hundred years, so little changed in its original constitution and appearance, as that of St. Cross.

* From *The Hampshire Chronicle.*

The Domus Dei, Southampton, St. Cross Hospital in this city, in common with other foundations of those days, united the entertainment of travellers, with the care of the sick.

The Hospital represents two distinct Foundations—that of Bishop de Blois (1136) and of Cardinal Beaufort (1444).

Bishop De Blois' Foundation.

St. Cross Hospital was founded in the year 1136, by Henry de Blois (Bp. of Winchester, and brother of King Stephen) for thirteen decayed men, past their strength.

The brethren live in the thirteen houses, each of which has two rooms, a pantry, and garden. They wear a long black gown with a silver cross on the left breast, and each receives a weekly allowance in money, and a daily portion of meat, bread, and beer. On the chief Festivals they are regaled on 'plum porridge' and large mince-pies. After Morning Service on Good Friday they partake of a kind of batter, which is called 'Judas' sop.'

Formerly, besides these thirteen brethren, Bp. de Blois' foundation allowed that one hundred others—called 'the Hundred Hall Poor'—the poorest in the city, of good character, should be provided every day with a loaf of bread, three quarts of small beer, and two messes for their dinner, in a hall appointed for the purpose, called *Hundred Mennes-Hall;* and they were permitted to carry home with them whatever they did not consume.

Bp. de Blois' foundation also provided for a Master, with the salary of from seven to eight pounds annually, together with a steward, four chaplains, thirteen clerks, and seven choristers—the latter were kept at school in the Hospital. There were also maintained a porter, nine servants, two teams of six horses each, and two carters.

The Wayfarer's Dole.—The horn of beer and piece of white bread—given on knocking at the Porter's hatchway—is one of the last remaining instances of that olden-time charity which could make provision for all comers. Tickets to view the place are here obtained:—6d. for one, 1s. for three, and 1s. 6d. for a party—the money obtained is divided equally between the Exhibitor on duty for the month, the library, and the burial fund.

INTERIOR OF PORTER'S LODGE.

In consequence of the rapacity of several of the masters, the purposes of the charity were perverted; but, in 1371, Bp. Wm. of Wykeham, recovered much of the alienated property. The revenues of the Hospital, in Wykeham's time, are stated to have been £400 a year.

All that remains of the money for the Hundred Hall Poor is given in quarterly payments to certain poor in the parish of St. Faith, of which there is no church, the living being held with the Mastership of St. Cross. The ancient doles, on the

Feast of the Holy Cross (May 3), and on the obit. of the Founder (Aug. 9), and on the eves of the great festivals, having become much abused, are now confined to the brethren of the Hospital.

Cardinal Beaufort's Foundation for an Almshouse of Noble Poverty.

In 1444, Cardinal Beaufort (Bp. of Winchester), appointed, in addition to the number of persons upon the first establishment, two priests, thirty-five brethren, and three sisters, who were to act as nurses to the sick and infirm. He considerably enlarged the original buildings of the Hospital, which were henceforth called 'The Almshouse of Noble Poverty.'* Beaufort's endowments, however, soon became the prey of mercenary men, and on Henry VII's accession only sufficient funds remained for the support of a chaplain and two brethren.

The Hospital Property.

The Reformation in no way interfered with the Hospital; but in 1616 the charters and deeds are said to have been burnt by the widow of the then Steward (one Mr. Wright), to hide her husband's defalcations. During Cromwell's protectorate, the regicides, John Lisle and Cook (Solicitor to the Parliament), were Masters of the Hospital successively; and in 1667 the

* The following old account is extant which must have been made very soon after Beaufort's Almshouse was in full working order, in the time of Thomas Forrest, clerk, master of the house aforesaid, 1460. 'In payment to 38 brethren and sisters for their table by the year, to everyone receiving by the day 2d., £115. 11s.; in payment to the above said brethren and sisters for their stipends by the year, for everyone receiving by the year 26s. 8d., £50. 13s. 4d.; for five pieces of cloth and 15 yards of deep red cloth, for making 38 cloaks thereof in the said year, to every one a cloak, £14. 7s. 11d.; for five pieces of cloth of deep red colour, recoloured, together with the cutting of the same, £1. 2s.; for payment for making 38 cloaks, £1. 18s., for payment to William Bowden for making the cardinals' hats thereon, together with silver thread, black and white silk, 4 ells of silk and 1 ell of canvas, £1. 0s. 0d.; for payment of (Mason) for placing a new copper in the house of the sisters by the tank, 6d.; for payment to the clerks, brethren, and sisters, as well of the new foundation as of the old foundation, together with and the ringing of bells on the anniversary of the Lord Cardinal, the founder, £3. 5s. 3d.; for the expenses of John Lydeford, one of the brethren of the new foundation, in riding to (? London) on the business of his brethren, and his horse, two times, 3s. 4d.'

office was filled by the soldier priest, Henry Compton, who afterwards, as Bp. of London, crowned William and Mary.

In 1855, during the Mastership of the Earl of Guilford, after much litigation, the Court of Chancery approved a provisional scheme for management. The system of selling long leases of the charity lands for large sums, leaving only small rents for the support of the Hospital, is now forbidden ; and when some of the larger leases expire, the Trustees will doubtless be enabled to extend the usefulness of this ancient and far-famed Hospital. The value of the Hospital property by about the year 1912, when all the leases have fallen in, will be about £9,000 per annum.* When the Trustees were first appointed, the income of the Hospital was about £1700 per annum. The present income is between £3,000 and £4,000.

The Trustees are—

In 1877 a Committee of the Trustees of the Hospital recommended the following scheme for the application of the surplus income of the charity :—

PROPOSED SCHEME OF MANAGEMENT.

1.—That the separate existence of the two foundations of the Hospital of St. Cross and the Almshouse of Noble Poverty be clearly recognized.

2.—That the income from both foundations be considered as one applicable to the distinct purposes of either foundation.

3.—That both foundations be under the care of the Master of St. Cross, with the title of Master of St. Cross and Warden of the Almshouse of Noble Poverty.

THE HOSPITAL OF ST. CROSS.

4.—That the Hospital of St. Cross be managed with express reference to ts ancient purpose as a place of relief for the impotent and indigent poor.

* The ultimate incomes of Bp. de Blois' foundation of St. Cross Hospital, will amount to nearly £7000, and the income of Cardinal Beaufort's almshouse of Noble Poverty to nearly £3000.

5.—That the maintenance of the Hospital of St. Cross in its integrity be the first charge on the combined income, and that the number of these brethren be not less than thirteen.

6.—That the brethren be chosen from amongst the needy with express reference to their impotence and infirmity of body, in accordance with the original terms of the charter of the hospital, but that no brethren be chosen whose case presents either repulsive features or danger of contagion.

THE ALMSHOUSE OF NOBLE POVERTY.

7.—That your committee be empowered to consult Mr. Butterfield as to the best manner of appropriating, arranging, or restoring the present buildings, so as to retain suitable accommodation for the brethren of St. Cross, and to make due provision for the brethren and sisters of the Almshouse of Noble Poverty.

8.—That a complete plan be prepared for the whole of the works contemplated, so that the same may be carried out by degrees as funds may permit.

9.—That the brethren of the Almshouse of Noble Poverty be chosen from men who, by misfortune, have been reduced to poverty from more affluent circumstances.

10.—That the number of the brethren do not exceed thirty-five.

11.—That the brethren be provided with apartments, meat, bread, groceries, coal, cloaks, and money allowance, or with cloaks and money allowance only, as the trustees may determine.

12.—That they wear the cloak of the brotherhood within and without the precincts of the house, and that the cloak be of the ancient colour, dark red, with the badge of the brotherhood on the breast.

13.—That three sisters of the Almshouse of Noble Poverty be appointed to be chosen solely with the view to their employment as nurses in the infirmary, and as general assistants in case of sickness in the house and hospital.

14.—That they reside in the hospital or in the parish of St. Faith, until accommodation shall be provided for them in the hospital, but that the Master of St. Cross be permitted to employ them as nurses within the parish of St. Faith when not wholly employed within the house and hospital.

15.—That apartments be provided for them in the hospital, and that they be maintained in the same way as the brethren of the almshouse, and also have the cloak of the brotherhood.

16.—That a chaplain of the House of Noble Poverty be appointed, who shall act as the curate of the Master of St. Cross and Warden of the Almshouse of Noble Poverty, both within the almshouse and hospital, and generally in the spiritual care of the parish of St. Faith.

17.—That the appointment of brethren and sisters of the Almshouse of Noble Poverty proceed by degrees as funds permit, and as apartments are prepared for the occupation of the brethren.

18.—That no further elections be made to the Hundred Hall poor.

Other proposals have also been made as to the administration of the increasing funds of this Hospital.

THE PRESENT BUILDINGS.

In the OUTER COURT, on the left, are remains of an ancient building, probably a portion of the earlier building of St. Cross Hospital; and on the right the large kitchen offices, etc.

BEAUFORT'S TOWER (1404—97) rises above the roofing on either side, and its outline is relieved by a handsome octagonal turret with spiral stair. The vault of the gateway is richly groined, and over it is the Founder's chamber, or muniment room. The niche on the south exterior was formerly occupied by a figure of the Blessed Virgin, which fell nearly a century ago, almost crushing one of the brethren in its fall. This statue had been preserved from destruction by iconoclasts, through an invented story that it represented a milkmaid with a pail on her head. On the north side, the only remaining figure in the three niches is that of the Cardinal, in a kneeling posture. The central niche was originally filled with the Holy Cross, and in the other was a statue of the first Founder, Bp. Henry de Blois.

In the cornice on either side over the gateway is the Cardinal's hat, the busts of his father (old John of Gaunt, time-honoured Lancaster), of his royal nephews Henry IV and Henry V, and of his predecessor, Wykeham. The centre boss of the groining is a curious cross composed of leaves surrounded with a crown of thorns. In the spandrels appear the Founder's arms, viz., France and England quarterly. The gates are strictly barred at nine in the evening during the summer, and at eight in the winter. *(See Illustration.)*

Robert Sherburn, one of the Masters, inserted his favorite motto 'DELIXI SAPIENTIAM' with his initials and date, 1503, in the wall of the Porter's lodge.

The view, on passing through this gateway, is interesting. The grey masonry of the fine old Church fronting the tall trees and quiet meadows beyond, with the varied outline of the other buildings, is shewn to best advantage by the open square of well kept turf.

On the east is a low CLOISTER of the 16th century—one part of which affords an early specimen of brickwork—some of the bricks being of a very small make. One of the rooms in the upper part of the Cloister opens into the Church, whereby the sick had an opportunity of taking part in the Services. The solid oval table, in the lower walk, is said to have been brought from Winchester Castle.

THE CHURCH (A.D. 1171—1292) is one of the most interesting architectural studies. Good examples of every style—from Romanesque, Transition-Norman, and Early English to late Decorated are seen here. In Transition-Norman this Church is considered the best example in existence. Its height is good, and it has stone vaulting throughout. *(See Illustration.)*

Dimensions of the Church.

Extreme length, W. to E....	125 feet
,, breadth at Transepts	115 ,,
Nave and Aisles, breadth of	54 ,,
Nave, height of	57 ,,
Tower Lantern, inside height of	77 ,,

NOTES ON THE EXTERIOR.

In the Nave, the windows vary from Transition-Norman to Early English, and in the Clerestory become Decorated. The windows on the north side are the richest.

The only remaining portion of De Blois' Hospital is at the end of the South Transept. These remains prove that the original buildings were south of the Church; and this arrangement accounts for the plainness of the walls on this side.

Woodward thinks it probable, from the dimensions of the Transepts, and the squeezed appearance of the lower east window of the North Transept, that the body of the Church has been widened subsequently to its first erection by De Blois.

S. Cross Church

The walls and windows of the Choir Aisles are late Norman. At the end of the Church are square towers rising from flat buttresses.

The upper windows in the Choir and Transepts are of later date than the lower. In early times builders did not usually 'adopt' a style, but used or improved the style of their day: thus it is that the date of their work can generally be traced.

The workmanship of the western Early English doorway is excellent, and presents a good variety of tooth ornament. The nail head moulding, as on round window in eastern gable, was a first development of the tooth ornament.

The north porch is Early English.

The splendid geometrical tracery in the great western window is 'fully developed Decorated.'

In the south-east corner of the South Transept is a 'Triple-arch.' Probably it was a doorway into the Cloister, a portion of the Nave wall being cut away, in order that the door might open right in the angle, for some interior convenience.

The circular openings in the east gable (now glazed) were made to admit air to the roof timbers.

THE INTERIOR OF THE CHURCH is remarkable for the loftiness of its proportions and the rich ornamentation of its arches and mouldings. It has been carefully restored by Butterfield, and moderately colored. The simplicity of the vaulted ceiling should be noticed.

NOTES ON THE INTERIOR.

The western portion of the Nave is Early English; the bay next the Transepts is Transition-Norman.

Two fragments of a border, now placed in one of the North Transept windows, are considered by Winston to be the earliest glass in the neighbourhood, and to have come out of one of the Norman windows.

The bird's beak moulding in North Transept is worthy of notice.

The Font is said to have been brought from St. Faith's Church.

On the south wall of the South Transept is a fresco of the Descent from the Cross covering the whole of the wall; very indistinct. Not only can a portion of the representation of the Saviour be seen, but amongst other things, the tops of the houses at Jerusalem. The fresco could be seen from the upper cloister room which opened into the Church.

In the South Aisle (east end) is a Morning Chapel. The stalls here (temp. Hen. VIII.) were brought from the chancel.

The encaustic tiles bearing the appropriate motto for a house of prayer, 'HAVE MYNDE,' probably date from 1390. The new tiles are from the old designs. The letters Z.O. refer to the anonymous contributor to the recent restorations.

All round the Choir there is a second triforium, or passage, beneath the windows of the clerestory. The Choir roofs have been so lowered that the small pointed triforium windows can be seen outside.

Above the pier arches of the Choir is the celebrated triforium of intersecting arches to which Dr. Milner attributed the origin of the pointed style.

In the Choir the pointed arch is used throughout as an arch of construction, but the semi-circular arch is retained as an arch of decoration.

The carving in the Chancel is of about the period of Henry VII. The arrangement of windows in the east end is very effective.

At the base of the present Communion table is placed John de Campeden's (1392) original Purbeck Altar Slab, with its five consecration crosses, in good preservation.

The eagle and scroll on the small credence table doubtless refers to the Hospitallers of St. John, who were appointed by De Blois administrators of the charity.

John de Campeden's floor brass (1382) lies in the Choir.

A monument to Cornwall (speaker to the House of Commons 1789) is in the South Aisle. The mace appears on his monument because he died whilst actually holding the office of Speaker of the House of Commons, dying whilst in office entitling a Speaker to that distinctive mark.

In the south Choir Chapel are the following quaint records :—

'SUSANA LAVRENCE
VAS CARNE VALENS.
A FLESH-PREVAILING VESSEL FOVND
BEAVTIF'D TO LYE VNDER GROVND.
VIXIT DEC. 13, 1647.
DEVIXIT JAN. 18, 1650.'

'GEORGIVS LAVRENCE
EGO VTI LAVRVS RIGENS.
I VNDER LY
AS LAVREL DRY.
VIXIT OCTOB. 14, 1650.
DEVIXIT SEP. 19, 1651.'

THE HALL (originally part of the Hundred Mennes Hall, about thirty-six feet by twenty-four) has four rich Perpendicular windows, and at the east end a daïs for the table of officers—those for the Brethren being ranged along the sides. There is yet much to excite interest, and to convey an idea of its original appearance: the rude yet ornamental display of roof timbers, the gallery at the end, whence the benediction was given, and whence on festivals the cheerful sound of minstrelsy enlivened the banquet; a quaint fifteenth century staircase, and the raised hearth in the centre of the Hall, round which the Brothers are wont to sit on festivals, and awaken the listlessness of age by the memories of by-gone days.

THE HALL.

The Early English stained glass over the entrance shows the arms of England, conjoined to the lilies of France.

The black leathern jacks, the candlesticks, salt-cellars, pewter dishes, and dinner-bell, belong to Beaufort's time (1446).

On the east wall is placed an Early German triptych.

Under the hall is a groined cellar.

Many of the scenes in *Henry Dunbar* are represented as occurring in the village of St. Cross.

The Monument.

THE MONUMENT was erected shortly after the plague of 1666, during which the peasants brought food to this spot, depositing it on a stone near the top of the base on the southern side, from which it was taken by the townspeople when the former had left, the citizens also leaving the money in a bowl of water for the confiding countrymen; by this means infection was avoided. The Monument was rebuilt in 1758.

The Westgate.

THE WESTGATE is said to have been preserved (at the time when the other Gates were removed) through a chamber in it, over the gateway, being claimed by the owner of the adjoining house on the south side. It is an excellent specimen of defensive architecture, portions of which are ascribed to King Stephen, and others to a later date. *(See Illustration.)*

The last of the other three Gates of the City was removed in 1780. They were such low structures that their removal was necessary. In early times persons passing in or out of the City had to pay toll at these gates: the money went to the king.

The Barracks.

THE BARRACKS were commenced in 1683, on the site of the old Castle, by Charles II, as a royal palace, from a design by Sir C. Wren. After two years, the work was stopped on account of the death of the king. The portion erected was fitted up as a depôt for prisoners of war, and a large number of refugee French priests were here quatered. In 1796 the buildings were first used as permanent barracks, and to these there has been added officers' quarters, military hospital, barrack for married soldiers, schoolroom and stores.

The Great Hall of Winchester Castle.

[To view the Hall, apply at the Tower doorway.]

THE GREAT HALL* forms the only portion now existing of the old Castle, which was one of the fortresses built by William the Conqueror, and the records of which show that it has been the scene of great and important events.

It was the principal residence of William, and of all the Plantagenet kings.

Hence Rufus started on that hunting expedition from which he never returned.

Here Henry I celebrated his marriage with Matilda of Scotland.

Cœur-de-Lion was received at the Castle by all his nobles when he returned from his treacherous captivity.

Henry III was born in this Castle.

All the Edwards held court here.

Henry V received the ambassadors of Charles of France in the Castle.

* MR. MELVILLE PORTAL has entrusted to Messrs. Pickering the publication of an exhaustive and elaborate *History of the Great Hall of Winchester Castle.*

Henry VI constantly resided here, and here matured his plan for the foundation of Eton, on the model of Wykeham's School.

Here Arthur, son of Henry VII, was born.

Here Henry VIII entertained the Emperor Charles V.

Here Mary received Philip, and concluded their ill-omened nuptials.

Close at hand Charles II built his great palace, intending to reside there.

The Hall is about 111 ft. 3 in. in length, and 55 ft. 6 in. in width. It was originally Norman, but was altered into the Early English style of architecture by Henry III, and again further transformed by Richard II. In it the Parliaments of England sat for nearly 400 years. The king's commission has been executed there for upwards of three centuries, and some of the most important laws have been passed, and some of the greatest trials heard in it.

The Hall has been recently restored under the direction of Mr. Portal, of Laverstoke, now Chairman of Quarter Sessions. The southern door is in its original place, and there are traces of a doorway facing it on the opposite side. A small doorway at the east end of the north wall, still discernable, led originally to the buttery and kitchens. Opposite to this is a recess which was the lavatory, an appendage common to halls of this period, of which there is another fine example at Dacre Castle, in Cumberland.

The columns, which support the roof, are all of Purbeck marble, and the arrangement of the Hall is one common to halls in the early part of the thirteenth century. Westminster Hall originally had similar columns, although almost all trace of them has long since disappeared. The Hall at Oakham is built precisely on the same plan, and another at Angers, built by Henry II of England, is divided into side aisles and nave in centre, and supported by clustered columns, just like the County Hall.

The roof has been faithfully restored, the radiated roses in it being those of Edward IV.

The windows are considered to be among the finest specimens of early thirteenth century windows. In one of the southern windows are still to be seen the hooks to which the shutters were hung. So late as 1688 it was found that only the upper parts of windows were glazed even in king's palaces, and these shutters were used to keep out the weather. They were the property of the tenant and treated as movable fixtures, and were thought to be a luxury, not a necessity of life!

At the west end of the Hall is a very fine original doorway, which formerly led to the private chambers of the king.

The old remains of the wall preserved at the west end formed, no doubt, the daïs on which the king sat, delivered judgment, and listened to the debates of the Parliament in the Hall. Above it is a trough, or perthisis, which ran through the wall, and enabled the king from the solar chamber, or private apartments, to hear what was going on in Parliament, as he sat in his chamber.

The Hall was the property of the Crown till the time of James I, when it was granted to one of the Tichborne family, from whom it passed to Sir William Waller, who sold it as a public Hall for the county, to which it has ever since belonged.

ARTHUR'S ROUND TABLE.

The 'round table,' supposed to be King Arthur's, is formed like a cart wheel. It has been repaired two or three times, and there is no doubt, from its structure, that it was really a table, round which people sat.

History shows that it was considered as a curiosity in the time of Henry VI. It must, therefore, be 400 years old, and it is highly probable that it is 600.

This table was repainted temp. Henry VIII, and since then the same style has been repeated.

The county authorities have been anxious that the Hall should be a chronicle of the county history, and for that purpose they have availed themselves of the opportunity to introduce into the windows the arms of all the distinguished men connected with the county, from the earliest time, to the time of Charles II, when the Hall ceased to be the property of the Crown.

On the eastern wall are placed the names of knights of the shire, and in the inner Hall the names of the sheriffs from the earliest date till now. Beyond them, again, in the corridor between the two Courts, are the arms of the Lords Lieutenant, so that there is, in this building, a complete history of Hampshire recorded on the walls by means of its architecture, or through its decorations. Such a history so recorded, is probably unique, in this or any other country; and Mr. Melville Portal has, by this restoration, contributed one of the most valuable, and at the same time, one of the most interesting memorials of our county.

The Westgate, Winchester.—A. D. 1154.

RUINS OF HYDE ABBEY 1815.

A brief notice of Hyde Abbey.

THE far-famed, and at one time the enormously wealthy, Hyde Abbey,* is reached from Jewry street. It was built by King Henry I and Bishop William Giffard, in Hyde Mead, outside the north gate of the City, to replace the New Minster, which had been founded by King Alfred the Great, inconveniently near to the Cathedral. The abbot and monks took possession of their new buildings in Hyde Meads in 1110, and removed with them, not only the relics of the saints, but the remains of King Alfred himself, and other illustrious dead. The Abbots of Hyde were afterwards honoured with a mitre, and a seat in Parliament as peers of the realm.

The following is a brief account of some of the more prominent events in the history of the Abbey, and is compiled from the *Liber de Hyda*, *Milner's History*, etc.

A.D. 1041, the Dowager Queen Emma gave to the New Minster the head of St. Valentine (who was decapitated in Rome, A.D. 270), which relic was placed with the remains of St. Josse and St. Grimbald, in the silver shrine attached to the altar.

A.D. 1066, Abbot Elfury, brother of Earl Godwin, induced twelve of his stalwart monks, with a score of men-at-arms, to follow him to the field of Hastings, where they fell (but only as

* For a complete history of this renowned Abbey, see *Liber de Hyda*, published by Longman.

Hampshire men) almost to a man. As a punishment for their opposing valour, the Conqueror seized 17,000 acres belonging to the fraternity; and suffered two years to pass before he would allow a new abbot to be elected, during which time the property of the monastery lay at the mercy of the Norman nobles. The Conqueror himself seized part of the monastic enclosure, and thereon erected a new portion to his older royal palace; he further seized a splendid jewelled cross given by Canute. Eventually the cross was restored, and restitution was made of some of the manors.

According to Domesday Book it is estimated the Abbey owned 17,000 acres in Hampshire, and over 10,000 in Wiltshire, besides other large possessions.

A.D. 1141, during the civil wars of Stephen's time, Hyde Abbey was partially burnt down. Among the precious ashes were 'sixty pounds in weight of silver; fifteen pounds in weight of gold; three diadems, adorned with precious stones; two golden images of the Virgin and of St. John,—one of which the bishop stripped of its gold and gems; two silver patens, handsomely ornamented with gold; two very precious and richly adorned lavers, of the sort called "Salomonic" (as being made, it may be supposed, after the pattern of those of the Jewish temple); a silver vase for holy water, given by Cnut; with numerous other precious vases, censers, reliquaries, and the like.' Twenty-six years after its destruction, Bishop Henry de Blois caused a skilful restoration of this cross to be made.

A.D. 1267, a riot occurred between the servants of the Abbot, and those of the Pope's legate, Otho, who had come with a great retinue to keep Christmas. The festivities were carried out in such a manner as to lead to the Abbey being laid under interdict for four weeks.

A.D. 1415, Cardinal Beaufort obtained a verdict against the Abbot of Hyde on a plaint for obstructing the course of the Itchen.

A.D. 1445, a fine bell-tower, with its eight bells, was destroyed by fire.

A.D. 1522, complaints were made of the practice, by the junior monks, of long-bow archery in Hyde Meads; of keeping late hours—sitting for discussion to the hour of eight in the evening, and even later, instead of going to bed immediately after supper according to the wont of their order.

A.D. 1538, John Salcot, the last Abbot, surrendered the Abbey to King Henry VIII. He had previously been raised to the See of Bangor, and the year following his compliance was rewarded by his translation to the Bishopric of Salisbury.

In September, 1538, the Royal Commissioners, appointed to enforce the dissolution of the monastery, report to Thomas Cromwell:—'From Winchester this Saturday morning . . . . . About three o'clock a.m., we made an end of the shrine here at Winchester. . . . We think the silver thereof will amount to near two thousand marks . . . . Going to our beds-ward, we viewed the altar, which we purpose to bring with us . . . . Such a piece of work it is that we think we shall not rid it, doing our best, before Monday next or Tuesday morning. Which done, we intend both at Hyde and at St. Mary's to sweep away all the rotten bones that be called relics, *which we may not omit, lest it should be thought that we came more for the treasure than for avoiding the abominations of idolatory.*'

The Abbey was valued before the dissolution at £865. 18*s.* 0*d.* per annum. The monastic buildings appear to have been shortly afterwards pulled down, though considerable ruins remained till the County Bridewell was erected on their site, in the latter part of the last century.

Of all the possessions of Hyde Abbey, the Manor of Woodmancote, and that of Piddletrenthide, in Dorset, alone continue to be devoted to the promotion of education and piety, according to King Alfred's dearest hopes. These manors are now held by Winchester College, which obtained them from Henry VIII by exchange of other lands.

Nothing now remains above ground of this magnificent edifice but some out-buildings, used for farm purposes, entered by an arched gateway with canopy or hood-moulding, supported

F 2

by two crowned figure heads, said to represent Alfred and his son Edward. This gateway is nearly opposite to the lower entrance to the churchyard.

The foundations of the Abbey Church and its conventual buildings still exist *underground*, and are traceable whenever the surface is disturbed. Some chalk coffins were laid bare during the sewerage excavations.

That the body of the illustrious Alfred is here buried cannot be doubted ; but whether the remains repose undisturbed, or whether they are those which were disinterred some years ago, and now rest under a flat slab immediately to the east of the parish Church, remains an open question.

It is much to be regretted that an ancient stone, with the King's name inscribed upon it in Saxon characters, and supposed to be part of the base of a statue, or of the upper slab of his tomb, was suffered to be removed, in days gone by, to Corby Castle, Cumberland, where it is believed to be now preserved.

At any rate, the very circumstance of Alfred's burial in this spot, invests the immediate surroundings of Hyde Church with peculiar interest, and it is strongly felt that there is still wanting, on this spot, a direct memorial in some degree worthy of the immortal Alfred.

HYDE CHURCH, 1780.

The Parish Church of St. Bartholomew

STANDS a little removed from Hyde street, by the side of the road called King Alfred Place. It contains many Norman details, and is sometimes said to have been built with the stone supplied from the ruined Abbey; but, though it may have been enriched with some of the spoil, and the western tower would appear to be of the period of the dissolution, we think the Church may well claim to be an original building of considerable antiquity. The historian Milner, conjectured that it was formerly used for the servants and other lay persons belonging to the adjacent Abbey. In a recent enlargement, by which the north nave aisle was carried on to the western tower, and the Church considerably improved, the remains of Norman arch mouldings were discovered embedded in the wall, and these have been not only copied in the fresh work, but themselves re-used.

In the south porch, by the side of the enriched Norman doorway, may be seen a good example of an old stoup for holy water, recently discovered during the sewerage excavations, and placed in its present position as an interesting relic of the old Abbey.

The City of Winchester.

WINCHESTER, twelve miles north-east of Southampton, and sixty-two miles from London, chiefly occupies the eastern slope of a hill on the right bank of the Itchen.*

Area of city, 1,077 acres; population (1881), 18,667; number of burgesses, 2,413; Parliamentary Electors, 2,008; inhabited houses (1881), 3,213; rateable value of City, £71,166; total income of municipal authority, £15,600. Loans outstanding September 1st, 1880, on public buildings, etc., £10,688; amount borrowed to carry out drainage works, £37,500.

A moderate walk to St. Giles' Hill (at the foot of the High Street) gives the best view of the City, and a fine view in profile is gained from St. Catherine's Hill.

A Short History of Winchester.

'Memories from that long-faded land; the realm of Nevermore.'

B.C. 900.—This City is one of the most ancient in all England; in fact, its actual history is older than the authentic history of England itself. Its annals date from B.C. 900, when probably the first settlers came from the opposite coast of France.

* A river twenty miles long, formed by several streams which unite in the neighbourhood of Alresford. The river's course is westerly towards Winchester, and thence southerly to Southampton. There is also the Southampton and Winchester, or the Itchen Canal, which is one of the most ancient in the kingdom. It was constructed in the reign of King John, and originally reached Alresford, but the navigation now ceases at Winchester. The canal generally follows closely the course of the Itchen, but does not coincide with the bed of the river.

These were followed by a German tribe called the Belgæ, who, as in other instances, named the place *Cæer Gwent*, or The White City.

B.C. 500, Dunwallo Mulmutius built walls enclosing the City in the form of a square.

B.C. 54, the legions of Julius Cæsar visited the City; and, about A.D. 48, the Emperor Vespasian, accompanied by his son Titus, first brought into subjection the territory of which Winchester was the capital, and named the City *Venta Belgarum*. The City was then in the form of a square, with walls of flint and mortar, vestiges of which remain; also a portion of a Roman road*—(it now leads to Tegg Down and onward). The City at this time was celebrated for its magnificent embroideries, wrought chiefly for the imperial court; here also, the tackling and sails of the Roman fleet, on the British coast, were almost exclusively prepared. A school for the instruction of priests in heathen mythology was maintained in Winchester.

A.D. 513, the City was taken by the Saxons, under the command of Cerdic, who landed in Hamble Creek; its former names were lost in that of *Wintanceaster* (the City of the Winte) now contracted into Winchester.

A.D. 800, in the Cathedral, Egbert was the first king crowned as king of all England.

A.D. 890, King Alfred, at the royal palace in this City, made his wise laws, and compiled his great survey of the kingdom—the first that had been made.

A.D. 896, after King Alfred's return from Rome, he established a Scriptorium in the New Minster. One beautiful specimen of Winchester illuminating at this date, is the *Golden Book of Edgar*.

* From this road can be seen the highest ground in Hampshire—Siddown Hill, 943 feet high, forming part of the North Down range, and is included in Highclere Park, the seat of the Rt. Hon. the Earl of Carnarvon; it is wooded to its summit. Beacon Hill, 900 feet, and Ladle Hill, near to Siddown, have Roman remains. Also within view, is Butser Hill, 917 feet, and old Winchester Hill, both part of the South Down range, the latter having remains of a Roman summer camp.

A.D. 925–940, during the reign of Athelstan, six mints were established in Winchester, whilst London had only three.* A story of these times, confirmed by the *Liber de Hyda*, relates how, after the City had been besieged for two years by the Danes, it was agreed that a single combat should decide by which side the victory should be claimed. Guy, Earl of Warwick, was the Saxon champion, who was assisted by a friendly crow, which fluttered about Colbrand, the Danish giant, and furthered his overthrow. Seeing their champion was dead, the hosts of northmen withdrew. The combat took place near Hyde Abbey, the site being still called Danemark; and was viewed by King Athelstan from a turret of the City wall (now destroyed) called Athelstan's chair.

A.D. 960, Edgar, who resided in the City, ordered standard vessels to be made and deposited here, and enacted that the *Winchester measure*,† should be observed throughout his dominions. One of his regulations appears singular. The Danes, being addicted to excessive drinking, it became a subject of frequent contest between them and the English at taverns, who could drink the deepest out of the ordinary drinking jug which passed throughout the company; Edgar made an ordinance, that certain pegs should be placed at equal distances, within all such vessels, forbidding any person to drink below his proper peg.

A.D. 1017–1035, Canute, who resided here, placed his royal crown over the crucified figure on the high altar in the Cathedral, after rebuking the flattery of his courtiers at Southampton. Canute, among other bestowals to the Cathedral Church of Winchester, gave the lands called 'Hille,'—probably St. Catherine's Hill.

A.D. 1042, Edward the Confessor was crowned in Winchester Cathedral, by Eadsinus of Canterbury, this being the first instance on record of a coronation sermon. When keeping Easter in the Great Hall of Winchester Castle, with Earl Godwin and other nobles, the butler, in carrying a dish, slipped

* Five of these were abolished by Henry I; the sixth remained till Henry III.

† Edgar's measures are still to be seen in the Winchester Museum at the Guildhall.

with one foot, but recovered with the other. 'Thus,' said Godwin, in a sportive vein, 'does one brother assist another.' This speech recalled to the king's mind the suspicion, that the Earl had caused the death of his brother Alfred. Accordingly he answered, in a tone of severity, 'So might I have been now assisted by my brother, Alfred, if Earl Godwin had not prevented it.' On this the Earl, holding up the morsel he was about to eat, pronounced a curse, and imprecated the vengeance of Heaven upon himself, that it might choke him if he was guilty of that murder. He put the meat into his mouth, and attempted to swallow it; but in vain—it stuck fast in his throat, his eyes became fixed, his body convulsed, and he fell dead under the table. The king, seeing divine justice thus manifested, commanded his servants to 'carry away that dog, and bury him in the high road.' His sons, however, took care to have him privately interred in the Cathedral.

A.D. 1017, Robert, Edward the Confessor's counsellor, afterwards Archbishop of Canterbury, having accused Emma, mother of Edward, of criminal intimacy with Alwyn, Bishop of Winchester, and with being accessory to the death of her son, Alfred; he seized all her treasures in this City, and compelled her to retire to the neighbouring convent of Wherwell. Emma wrote to different prelates insisting on undergoing the fiery ordeal, usual in those days, as a proof of her innocence. This being accepted, she came to the Cathedral, and, having spent the previous night in prayer, walked bare-footed over nine red-hot plough-shares, placed in the nave of the Cathedral, without suffering injury. An immense concourse witnessed her triumph. She died 1052, and was buried in the Cathedral.

A.D. 1069, the splendour of Winchester was rather increased by the Norman Conquest. William the Conqueror was crowned here for a second time. Here the chief mint, royal treasury, and public archives, particularly *Rotulus Wintoniensis* (called Domesday Book) were kept, and here the Conqueror and his sons, Rufus and Henry I, were wont to keep Easter with great pomp. During the Norman period, the City was populous and extensive—its suburbs reaching a mile every way beyond their present limits—on the north, to Worthy; on the west, to Week; on the south, to St. Cross; and on the east, to St. Magdalen's hill. It was the general thoroughfare from the eastern to the western parts of the kingdom, and was resorted to, from all parts, on account of its celebrated fairs. It had a considerable woollen manufactory, particularly in men's caps, and an extensive commerce with the neighbouring continent.

A.D. 1100, Henry I here married Matilda, the niece of Edgar, who had lived as a nun in St. Mary's Abbey, at Winchester, and here was born their son, Prince William, who early lost his life in attempting to save his sister from shipwreck.

A.D. 1135, Stephen, on his usurpation, was crowned here. During the Civil War, in 1141, a fire destroyed the greater part of the City, including forty churches and two abbeys. During the siege of the City, the Empress Matilda and her party were confined to the Royal Castle of Winchester, in which they might have bidden defiance to their enemies, had they not been straitened for want of provisions, and still more for want of water. The besiegers, having cut off the stream which encircled the fortress, brought matters to a crisis with the besieged, whose chief object was to save the person of Matilda, the empress. Here her genius came in aid of her valour. She caused a report to be spread of her illness, and then of her death. She was inclosed in a coffin of lead, and suffered to pass through the army of the besiegers in a litter, as if for interment—a truce being granted for the purpose. When arrived at a proper distance, she was freed from her enclosure, mounted a horse, and made the best of her way to Gloucester.

A.D. 1166, Henry II, finding the air of Winchester beneficial to his health, rebuilt the royal castle, and here summoned a council to deliberate on the invasion of Ireland.

A.D. 1184, the City was incorporated by Henry II, who granted a charter to it, a privilege London did not possess until twenty-two years later. Here he entertained Malcolm, King of Scotland; here his daughter Maud, with her husband Henry, Duke of Saxony, was received by him; and here, also, the duchess gave birth to a son, who was named William, from whom the House of Brunswick and the present reigning family descended.

A.D. 1194, Richard I (*Cœur de Lion*), after his return from his German prison, hastened to Winchester, and caused an inventory to be made of the treasures deposited in the exchequer here. The amount exceeded £900,000 in gold and silver, besides costly vessels, jewels, and precious stones. Here he received the homage of his nobility, and here he was crowned with unusual magnificence. The coronation dinner was cooked in the Refectory of St. Swithun's Monastery, a finely vaulted chamber now forming the kitchen to a house on the west side of the close. In this reign, Bishop Godfrey de Lucy restored the Navigation of the Itchen from Southampton to Alresford, where by the construction of a reservoir (Alresford pond) he provided for the regulation of the stream.

A.D. 1207, King John visited Winchester, and held a Parliament of the chief men of the kingdom, for the purpose of imposing a tax. In October of the same year, his queen, Isabella, was delivered of a son, who, from his birthplace, was surnamed *Henry of Winchester*. King John, after his excommunication by the Roman pontiff, was absolved in the Chapter House of Winchester Cathedral.

A.D. 1216, Henry III, during his long minority, appears to have held his Court frequently in Winchester, his native City, under the guardiancy of Bishop Peter de Rupibus.

A.D. 1249, on the death of Peter de Rupibus, followed a conflict between Henry III and the monks of the Cathedral. The king was desirous of appointing William of Valencia, the uncle of his newly-married queen, to the episcopal throne of Winchester, while the monks were bent on refusing his choice. The dispute lasted for five years; and though the Chapter suffered stripes, imprisonment, and famine, they maintained their right, and elected William de Raley for their Bishop. This prelate, coming to Winchester to take possession of his charge, found all the gates of the City shut against him. He walked around the walls, preaching to the magistrates on the duty of receiving their duly-appointed pastor, but all to no purpose. At last, taking his station at the King's gate, he fulminated an interdict upon the Cathedral and all the other churches, and an excommunication against the mayor and bailiffs, and all the clerks, etc., who opposed his entrance. The Bishop then withdrew to France; but was soon after restored to his diocese, and the favour of the king.

A.D. 1265, during the Baron's war, Winchester was sacked by the younger de Montfort. Edward I, in 1274, bestowed a new seal on the corporation. An old seal of this date is still preserved. A parliament was held during the king's visit—which lasted more than three weeks. Edward I, at the same time, received the submission of Gaston de Bierne, one of his foreign vassals, who had rebelled; he was conducted to the king with a halter round his neck. In the year 1279 Edward I resided here for six months. Half-pennies and farthings were first coined in Winchester, during this reign.

A.D. 1285, a parliament was held, in which certain ordinances were instituted,—afterwards known as *The Statutes of Winchester*,—for the security of persons and property. The great fair held on St. Giles' hill (where formerly stood St. Giles' chapel, and where, in A.D. 1076, Earl Waltheof was beheaded for conspiring against the Conqueror) attracted merchants from every part of Europe. The original charter for holding the fair was granted by William the Conqueror to Bishop Walkelin, and the transaction of business was strictly forbidden at Southampton and every place within seven leagues of the City. For several centuries this fair was by far the most considerable fair held in the kingdom. The streets of booths were named: the streets of the Flemings, of Caen, of Limoges, of Genoese; there were also streets called the Stannary, the Drapery, the Spicery, the Pottery, etc. The fair attracting bands of outlaws from all parts of the country, mounted sergeants-at-arms carefully guarded the roads for a great distance. The fair commenced on the Feast of St. Giles' (Sept. 1st), and, for the preservation of order, a court called the 'pavilo' was appointed. William Rufus extended the fair to three days, Henry I to eight, Stephen to fourteen, and Henry III to sixteen days. The fair has for years been abolished.

A.D. 1305, the royal favour which Winchester had enjoyed was lost by the escape from the Castle of Bernard Pereres, a foreign hostage of high rank. The king required the mayor, bailiffs, and six aldermen to appear before him at the Parliament at Westminster. They were committed close prisoners in the tower, and fined three hundred marks. By another writ, he ordered the sheriff to seize upon the city, and declare all its liberties disannulled. But, by the persevering intercession of Queen Margaret, the fine was remitted, the magistrates enlarged, and the privileges of the City restored. The queen, greatly endeared to the citizens by her gracious interposition, resided here during the absence of the king in Scotland, and was here delivered of the princess Eleanor.

A.D. 1327, shortly after the murder of Edward II, Queen Isabel and Mortimer held a Parliament at Winchester, where the exemplary Earl of Kent, was attainted of high treason, and condemned to death. In the morning he was brought to the scaffold, before the castle-gate, but no person could be induced to perform the office of headsman. The earl remained on the scaffold till evening, when a criminal from the gaol, in order to save his own life, beheaded him.

A.D. 1340, by an order of this date, the following tithe was demanded :—'Every non-freeman shall pay, for every cart-load of salmon brought into Winchester, *3d.* ; for a horse-load, *2d.* ; for what a man carries, *1d.*'

A.D. 1363, Edward III removed the wool trade to Calais. The result was an emigration of the inhabitants, so that the streets were deserted, the navigation neglected, and the City wore the aspect of decay.

A.D. 1388, Richard II and his Queen visited Winchester ; and in 1392 Richard removed his Parliament from London to Winchester.

A.D. 1399, Henry IV having contracted a match with Joan, dowager duchess of Brittany, chose to meet her in this City, and to have the magnificent ceremony of his marriage performed in the Cathedral.

A.D. 1406, Henry V was chiefly educated at Winchester College, and New College, Oxford. Previous to embarking for the coast of France, Henry received the Archbishop of Bruges and the other ambassadors of the French king, in this City.

A.D. 1449, Henry VI held a Parliament here, from the 16th of June to the 16th of July. In a petition presented to his Majesty, at this time, we learn that 997 houses were destitute of inhabitants, and that seventeen parish churches were shut up—evincing the rapid decline of the city.

A.D. 1487, Henry VII, believing the castle of Winchester had been built by his supposed ancestor King Arthur, brought hither his queen, Elizabeth of York, to be delivered of his eldest son, whom he named Arthur.

A.D. 1522, Henry VIII visited Winchester, where, in company with the Emperor Charles V, he spent a week in viewing its antiquities. On the dissolution of the religious houses, the City suffered great losses. The properties of the following minor establishments were first seized:—

The Sustern Spital or Convent of Hospitable Nuns, near Kingsgate;
The Carmelites, in Kingsgate Street;
The Augustines, near the Southgate;
The Dominicans, at Eastgate;
The Franciscans, in Middle Brook Street.

Subsequently—

The Priory of St. Swithun was suppressed, and its revenues, valued at £1508, were, for the most part, applied to the support of the Cathedral;
The royal Abbey of Hyde, founded by Alfred the Great, was suppressed;
St. Mary's Abbey, Colebrook Street, endowed by Alfred's Queen, was suppressed;
The Hospital of St. Cross appears not to have been interfered with;

The College of St. Mary Winton was ultimately saved from the forfeiture of its property;
The Hospital of St. Mary Magdalene lost some of its possessions;
The College of St. Elizabeth was suppressed;
The Hospital of St. John the Baptist had all its property confiscated.

A.D. 1554, on the 25th July, the marriage ceremony between Philip of Spain and Mary was celebrated in the Lady Chapel in the Cathedral, with great pomp, by Bishop Gardiner. On this occasion, the queen compelled the restitution of all the lands alienated from the bishopric in the two preceding reigns, and a restoration of all the ornaments and moveable property, which could be found, previously taken from the Cathedral. The queen was anxious to restore likewise the whole of the abbey lands which had been seized upon by her father, Henry VIII; but this was found impracticable. The only original charitable establishment actually restored, during the short interval that the Catholic party was triumphant, was the Hospital of St. John the Baptist, which was new founded by Richard Lamb. During the persecutions under Mary, Thomas Benbridge, a person of some consideration, and a resident of this City, was burnt to death for holding opinions contrary to the faith of the prevailing party.

A.D. 1555, John Philpot, B.C.L., a native of Compton, educated at Winchester College, was burned at Smithfield, December 18th, for giving public lectures on St. Paul's Epistle to the Romans, and therein asserting the principles of the Reformation.

A.D. 1558, on the accession of Elizabeth, Bishop White was the first victim of the Oath of Supremacy. Hence he and Watson, Bishop of Lincoln, were first committed to the Tower. In June, 1559, he objected to take the Oath, and consequently forfeited his bishopric, which was kept vacant for a long time. The deposed bishop died January 11, 1560, and was at his own desire buried in the Cathedral. Among others who refused to acknowledge the Queen head of the Church, and who were consequently deprived of their livings, were Edmund Steward, D.D., the Dean of the Cathedral; Thomas Harding, D.D., the antagonist of Bishop Jewel; Peter Langrish, Prebendary of the Cathedral; Thomas Martin, LL.D., Chancellor of the Diocese; Thomas Hyde, D.D., Head Master of Winchester College, and Prebendary of the Cathedral; John Marshall, LL.B., Second Master of the College; Edmund Marvyn, A.M., Prebendary; and Richard Martial, another Prebendary.

A.D. 1587, Elizabeth granted a new charter to the City. The Queen visited Winchester once during her progress in the south. Subsequently, Sir Francis Walsingham, Secretary of State, assented to be chosen High Steward of the City; through whom a new charter was obtained, being the last with which the City has been privileged.

A.D. 1588, amongst the ancient privileges of Winchester was that of keeping the standard weights and measures; and, at this date, a new set of these were sent, marked with the arms and name of the Queen. One of these, which is a yard, bears the marks of Henry VII at one end, and those of Elizabeth, on a piece let into it, at the other end. Milner states that the length of the yard may have been altered at this period.

A.D. 1603, James I was proclaimed here on the sole authority of Sir B. Tichborne, who anticipated the commands of the Privy Council. The plague being rife in London, the king resolved to hold his courts of justice in this City. By the middle of November, an assemblage of judges, peers, lawyers, etc., was convened in Winchester to try what was called 'Sir Walter Raleigh's conspiracy.' The persons first arraigned were Raleigh; the Hon George Brooke; Sir Griffin Markham; Sir Edwd. Parham; Anthony Copley, and Barthol. Brooksby, Esqs.; Wm. Watson and Wm. Clarke, priests. All were condemned to death except Parham; but three of them only—viz., Watson, Clarke, and Brooke—were eventually executed. The priests, Watson and Clarke, were cruelly put to death, being cut down while yet alive. Lord Cobham and Lord Grey were also tried and condemned to suffer death; but, with Sir Griffin Markham, were pardoned at the hour appointed for their execution.

A.D. 1623, Taylor, the water poet, states that he found the city 'like a body without a soul,' with almost as many parishes as people.

A.D. 1637, Charles I and his queen visited Winchester, on which occasion the arms of the royal pair were put up in the hall of the Deanery, where they are still to be seen. Charles I levied £150 on the City as ship-money. During the contest between Charles and his Parliament, Winchester was the scene of much conflict.

A.D. 1644, on March 29, a great battle took place on Cheriton Down, where Waller routed the forces of Charles, many of whose officers were left dead on the field. From thence Waller advanced to Winchester, where his soldiers vented their rage against the monuments, images, vestments, and hallowed remains in the Cathedral.

A.D. 1645, after the battle of Naseby, Cromwell was sent to reduce the City and Castle to the authority of Parliament, which he executed with his wonted rapidity. Encamping on an eminence about a mile from the City, called 'Oliver's Battery,' he commenced firing into the City. Shortly afterwards he erected another battery nearer to the Castle, which, after a week's assault, surrendered on favourable terms. Cromwell blew up the Castle that it might not again be a retreat for royalists. The following letter contains Cromwell's account of the taking of the Castle :—

To the Right Honble. Sir Thomas Fairfax, General of the Parliament's Army.

Winchester, 6th October, 1645.

Sir,—I came to Winchester on Lord's day, the 28th Sept., with Colonel Pickering, commanding his own, Colonel Montague's, and Sir Hardress Waller's regiments. After some dispute with the Governor we entered the Town. I summoned the Castle; was denied; whereupon we fell to prepare batteries, which we could not perfect (some of our guns being out of order) until Friday following. Our battery was 6 guns, which being finished, after firing one round, I sent in a second summons for a treaty, which they refused. Whereupon, we went on with our work, and made a breach in the Wall near the Black Tower; which after about 200 shot we thought stormable, and purposed Monday morning to attempt it. On Sunday night, about 10 of the clock, the Governor beat a parley, desiring to treat. I agreed unto it; and sent Colonel Hammond and Major Harrison into him, who agreed upon these enclosed articles.

Sir, this is the addition of another mercy. You see, God is not weary in doing you good. I confess, Sir, His favour to you is as visible when He comes by His power upon the hearts of your enemies, making them quit places of strength to you, as when he gives courage to your soldiers to attempt hard things. His goodness in this is much to be acknowledged; for the Castle was well manned, with 680 horse and foot, there being near 200 gentlemen, officers and their servants; well victualled, with fifteen hundred weight of cheese, very great weight of meat and beer, near 20 barrels of Powder, 7 pieces of cannon; the works were exceeding good and strong. It is very likely it would have cost much blood to have gained it by storm. We have not lost twelve men. This is repeated to you, that God may have for it all his due. Sir, I rest, Your most humble servant,

Oliver Cromwell.

(Lieut.-Genl. Cromwell's Secty., who brings this letter, gets £50 for his good news.)

Wolvesey Castle was laid in ruins by Cromwell, and other fortifications appertaining to the City shared a similar fate. The Episcopal religion was suppressed, and the Presbyterian form established. A local tradition says Cromwell's soldiers made use of the Cathedral as a stable. The Church lands were sold, and the proceeds applied to government purposes.

A.D. 1648, on December 21, Charles was brought a prisoner to this City on his way to Windsor, and was received by the mayor, aldermen, and neighbouring gentry. About this time Captain Burleigh was tried here for an attempt to liberate the king, and being found guilty, was hanged and quartered.

A.D. 1666, the plague broke out in Winchester, proving dreadfully fatal to the inhabitants. A memorial of this sad visitation stands near the Westgate.

A.D. 1671, an act of Parliament was procured for restoring the navigation of the river from Southampton to Winchester.

A.D. 1682, Charles II, with his son James, frequently visited Winchester, where he took up his abode at the Deanery. He employed Sir C. Wren to draw a plan of a palace to be erected on the site of the demolished castle, and himself laid the foundation stone, March 23, 1683.

A.D. 1685, during the reign of James II, Mrs. Lisle, a respectable lady, was beheaded in the Market Square for harbouring persons disaffected towards the king. She was the widow of John Lisle, the famous regicide, a Master of St. Cross Hospital, and one of Cromwell's peers, who had previously represented Winchester in the Long Parliament. The jury acquitted her three times, but Judge Jefferies insisted on their pronouncing her guilty, and they at last complied.

A.D. 1686, William Lloyd, educated at Winchester College, Bishop of St. Asaph, Lichfield, and Worcester successively, was one of the seven bishops sent to the Tower by James II. Two other Wykehamists also were there with him, namely:—Ken, Bishop of Bath and Wells, and Turner, Bishop of Ely.

A.D. 1707, Queen Anne and her husband visited Winchester; and so pleased was the prince with its locality, that he resolved to finish the palace commenced by Charles II. Here again death interposed.

Among eminent natives of the City may be mentioned:—Wolstan, Bishop of Worcester; Dean Pace; Bishop Bilson, (Reviser of James' Bible); Dr. Lingard, (Historian). Edward Young (author of *Night Thoughts*) was born in the neighbouring village of Upham. Pope was educated at Twyford School (three miles distant). He was expelled for writing a satire on his master, who had turned papist. Amongst the men educated at Hyde Abbey School were—Admiral Lord Lyons, Lord Liverpool, Wolfe the Poet, Deans Gaisford and Garnier, George Canning, General Sir P. Maitland, and the Earl of Beaconsfield.

The George Hotel has existed on the same spot as the principal hostelry in the City for more than four hundred years.

St. John's Hospital.

THIS HOSPITAL, in the Broadway, was founded by St. Brinstan, Bishop, 931. It was refounded in 1289, by John Devenishe. In the reign of Henry VI Richard Devenishe founded and endowed the Chapel. At the Reformation all its property was confiscated, but the walls were left to the Corporation to erect a hall, etc.; a few beds were also left for poor people. In 1558, Ralph Lamb provided for the maintenance of six poor widows of citizens, etc. In the Hall the election of Mayor formerly took place; and in 1593, part of the building appears to have been used as a city prison. Portions of the ancient refectory may be traced under the hall. The buildings on the south side were erected in 1833, and the first houses on the north side in 1852. After twenty years' litigation, the old corporation surrendered the management of the Hospital, and Trustees were appointed under the Court of Chancery. The charity has been much impoverished, but, with good management, the funds have been largely increased, so that the present yearly income is nearly £2,000. The Chapel has been well restored.

Christ's Hospital.

THIS INSTITUTION is situate at the corner of Symonds' Street, and was founded in 1607 by Peter Symonds for the maintenance of six poor men, one matron, four boys, and two scholars at the Universities. The following inscription is on the building:—

CHRIST'S HOSPITAL,
Which was founded in the year of our Lord 1607,
By PETER SYMONDS, a Native of Winchester, and
afterwards a Mercer in the City of London.

The Endowments of this House are applied to the
Maintenance of Six Old Men, One Matron, and Four Boys;
And also to the Assistance of One Scholar
In each of the Two English Universities.
The Name
Of such a Benefactor
Is remembered with gratitude
by Posterity.

The old men wear gowns similar to the Brethren of St. Cross Hospital, but of a light blue colour.

Carlisle Memorial Home.

THIS HOME, founded in memory of the late Earl of Carlisle (a friend to Criminal Reform), was removed to Battery House, opposite the County Prison, from Queen's Square, Bloomsbury. Established in London, in 1865, to carry out the views expressed by the Royal Commissioners on Penal Servitude, it is designed as an Industrial Home for female convicts, who, by industry and good conduct, desire to be prepared for a return to a useful position in society.

There is accommodation in the Home for fifty inmates and three Matrons. One room is especially set apart as a Chapel. The inmates are employed in laundry and needlework, by supplies of which the public may assist the Institution.

The City Cross.

THE CITY CROSS was erected during the reign of Henry VI, by *The Fraternity of the Holy Cross*. An earlier market cross originally occupied the site. The present erection was repaired in 1835, and restored by Gilbert Scott in 1865.

The principal figures are :—

- William of Wykeham, with the statutes of his Colleges, and Pastoral Staff;
- Florence de Lunn, first Mayor of Winchester, 1184 ;
- King Alfred the Great ;
- The Martyr St. Lawrence (only *old* figure remaining).

In the top niches are eight figures, namely—SS. Thomas, Maurice, John, Peter, Lawrence, Bartholomew, Swithun, and the Blessed Virgin.

THE CITY CROSS.

In the year 1772, the commissioners of Pavement sold this ancient Cross to Mr. Dummer, of Cranbury Park, in this neighbourhood, who was preparing to remove it into his pleasure grounds; but the inhabitants generally, with a just indignation, drove away the workmen engaged for this purpose; and thus preserved this curious and interesting edifice.

St. Catherine's Hill.

ST. CATHERINE'S HILL was the stronghold of the old British city. There is a deep fosse around its summit, and on the highest point are the foundations of one of St. Catherine's hill-top chapels, commemorative of her remains being taken by angels to the top of Sinai. Near the clump of trees is a mismaze, said to have been cut on the turf by the college boy who wrote Dulce Domum; but antiquarians assert these labyrinths were made use of in the performance of certain penances for neglecting pilgrimages: hence their name *Chemins de Jerusalem*.

The Royal Hants County Hospital.

THIS HOSPITAL was established in 1736, in Colebrook Street, by Dr. Clarke, a Prebendary of the Cathedral, and was one of the first of its kind in England. A legacy from Richard Taunton, of Southampton, led to the erection of the old Hospital in Parchment Street. The new buildings on the West Hill were completed in 1868 from a design of Mr. Butterfield, at a cost of £30,000. The Hospital, which is supported by voluntary contributions, and contains 108 beds, is in need of larger funds.

Wolvesey Castle.

THE name appears to be a corruption of ULF'S (Wolf's), EY (Island). From early times it had been a stronghold of importance. In the seventh century Kinegils built here a Castle, which his son Kenewalch handed over to Bishop Agilbert (655). It has ever since belonged to the Bishop of Winchester.

The Castle, scanty ruins of which remain,* was built by Henry de Blois. The walls of the keep, and a great part of the outer walls are nearly perfect, and of good Norman character. 'The interior of the Castle affords little more than a very picturesque ruin; but considerable parts of the partition walls remain, and a part apparently of the refectory in which is

* The curious string courses in the walls, which take the place of the Roman bonding tiles, should be noticed. These bonding stones were probably brought from the old Saxon Royal Palace situate in the Square.

a good Norman arch and window.'* Some of the materials were brought from the old Royal palace in the Square. It stood a siege in the wars of Stephen and Matilda, was dismantled by Henry II and Henry III. For many years it was an ordinary residence of the Bishops of Winchester, and at one time was the seat of an episcopal seminary for the education of priests. Philip of Spain, stayed at Wolvesey when he came to Winchester to marry Queen Mary.

The Castle was destroyed by Cromwell in 1646; a modern house was afterwards built by Bishops Morley and Trelawny. Bishop North took down the greater part of this building, leaving one wing only standing with the Chapel, which is modern.

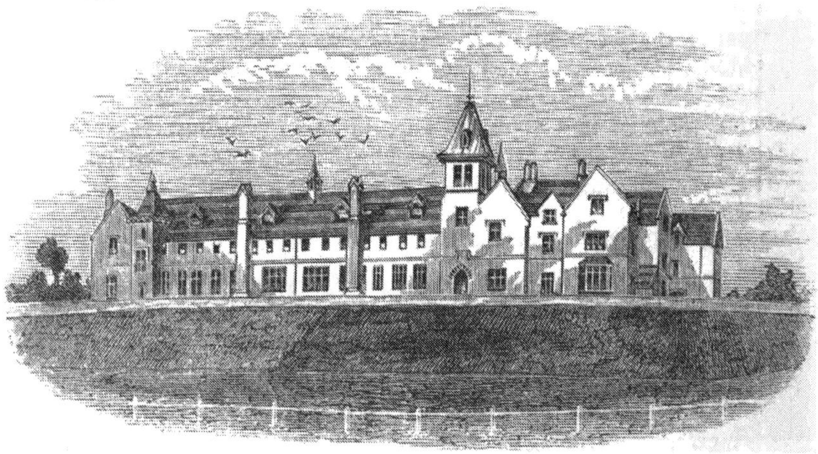

Winchester Diocesan Training College.

THIS COLLEGE is situate on the West Hill, and was erected in 1862, at a cost of about £8,000. A Memorial Chapel to the late Bishop of Guildford has since been built. The Dioceses of Winchester and Salisbury unite in this educational enterprise. The above is the College for Masters, and at Salisbury is a College for Mistresses.

* *Woodward*, p. 93.

The Guildhall.

THE GUILDHALL was erected in 1873, at a cost of £20,000. Forming the tympani of the windows are:—(1) Prince Arthur, A.D. 516, with his Paladins or Knights of the Round Table; (2) The Coronation of Egbert, A.D. 827; (3) Alfred the Great in Council here, A.D. 879; (4) Canute offering his Crown at the Altar of the Cathedral, A.D. 1015 (never worn after), placing it on the Holy Rhood; (5) William the Conqueror compiling Domesday Book, A.D. 1083; (6) Marriage of Philip and Mary in the Cathedral, July 25, 1554. The niches are filled with life-sized figures of Egbert, Alfred, (Saxon Kings armed), De Lunn, the first Mayor (holding the Charter), and Henry III. The heads on dripstone terminals, etc., represent:—Rufus, Edward the Confessor, Richard I, Elizabeth, Victoria, Dunwallo Mulmutius. The last named erected walls around the City B.C. 500. The subject of the alto-relievo under the belfry tower, is the presentation of the charter of incorporation to Florence de Lunn, in 1184, by Henry II. The front elevation is of Bath stone, red Mansfield bands and columns, Portland stone where necessary, and the columns in the vaulted entrance are porphyry polished. The clock is by *Jacob*, of Winchester; the five bells by *Warner*, of London. Height of tower, 112 feet.

The Museum.

THE CITY MUSEUM (at the Guildhall) is open daily from ten to three o'clock.

The School of Art and Free Library and Reading Room adjoin the Guildhall.

HAMPSHIRE FRIENDLY SOCIETY'S OFFICES.

The Hampshire Friendly Society.

THE Patron is H.R.H. ALBERT EDWARD PRINCE OF WALES, K.G. It was founded by John Fleming, Esq., in the year 1825, and has 8,236 Benefit, and 529 Honorary Members, with a capital of £70,311, and 82 Branches established throughout the County.

The Hospital of St. Mary Magdalene.

THIS HOSPITAL was similar in its charitable objects to St. Cross, and was situate on the downs near the milestone on the Alresford Road. It was founded by Bishop Toclyve (1173—89). William of Waynflete (1447—1486), afterwards Bishop, was formerly one of the Masters. Its funds were from time to time diverted, and at the Reformation it lost some of its property. During the reign of Charles I, the buildings were much damaged by the troops stationed there, and in the time of Charles II the Hospital was used for the confinement of Dutch prisoners. The ruins having become a refuge for beggars, they were removed in 1788. The present cottages in Water Lane were built in 1788. The Master is appointed by the Bishop of Winchester. The cottages are occupied by four men and four women, who receive a pension of two shillings a week. There is also an out pensioner. It is proposed to rebuild the Hospital.

The fine early Norman Gateway to the Catholic Chapel in St. Peter Street was removed from the ruins on Magdalene Hill. There is a fine Druidical cromlech, or altar stone, near this entrance.

Winchester Modern School.

Visitor—The Right Rev. The Lord Bishop of Winchester. Chairman of the Governing Body—The Right Hon. the Earl of Northbrook. Head Master—The Rev. John L. Ogle, M.A. Clerk—Henry White, Esq., 38, Jewry Street, Winchester.

Hursley—Merdon Castle, etc.

NEAR Hursley are the scanty remains of MERDON CASTLE, built by Bishop Henry de Blois in 1138. In the reign of Edward VI the manor of Merdon was surrendered to the crown by Bishop Poynet, and in the seventeenth century it became the property of Richard Cromwell, son of the Protector, through his wife's family. At his death, the manor was sold to the first Sir William Heathcote, who at once pulled down the old mansion, and during its destruction the seal of the Commonwealth was found hidden in the wall. In Hursley Church Richard Cromwell was buried; also the widow of Thomas Sternhold, who prepared with Hopkins the old verson of the Psalms, and who himself lived in the neighbouring village of Slackstead. The chief circumstance of interest in connection with Hursley is its association with the name of John Keble, author of *The Christian Year*, who, with his wife, is buried in the churchyard. Hursley Church was built out of the profits of *The Christian Year*, and the excellent stained glass windows were the contributions of readers of the work.

The SCHOOLHOUSE at Pitt was built, and the Church at Otterbourne was remodelled, at the cost of the authoress of *The Heir of Redclyffe*, who resides in the parish.

The Churches of Chilcomb (two and a half miles), Morestead (five miles), and Compton (two miles), should be visited by the antiquarian.

POPULATION OF WINCHESTER (1881).

St. Faith	2461	St. Michael	964
,, Thomas	3095	,, John	1258
,, Mary Kalendar ...	1247	,, Bartholomew Hyde ...	1432
,, Maurice	2504	Weeke	1809
,, Swithun	156	Winnall	124
,, Lawrence	224	Milland	255
,, Peter Colebrook ...	840	Barracks	1119
,, Peter Cheesehill ...	847	H.M. Prison	312

Within the Parliamentary Borough...	17690
Without the Parliamentary Borough	977
	18667

POPULATION OF NEIGHBOURING VILLAGES.

Bishopstoke	1537	King's Worthy	438
Chilcomb	300	Littleton	194
Compton	275	Lainston	15
Morestead	139	Martyr Worthy	249
Owslebury	848	Sparsholt	434
Twyford	1429	East Stratton	340
Avington	204	Hunton	69
Crawley	455	Micheldever	1041
Easton	484	Stoke Charity	116
Headbourne Worthy ...	242	Wonston	691
Itchen Abbas	244		

DISTANCES FROM WINCHESTER.

	Miles		Miles
ALRESFORD, NEW ...	8	Bishop's Sutton	9
Alresford, Old	9	Bishop's Waltham	10
ALTON	18	BOURNEMOUTH	41
Ampfield	7	Bramdean	9
ANDOVER	14	Bullington	8
Ashley	9	Candover, Brown	10
Avington	5	Candover, Chilton	11
Barton Stacey	8	Candover, Preston	13
BASINGSTOKE	18	Cheriton	8
Bighton	11	CHICHESTER	36
Bighton Wood	12	Chilbolton	10
Bishopstoke	7	Chilland	4

DISTANCES FROM WINCHESTER—*Continued.*

	Miles
Chilworth	9
Compton	3
Crawley	5
Curdridge	13
DORCHESTER	74
Droxford	14
Dummer	13
Durley	11
Easton	3
Ellisfield (or Illsfield)	14
FAREHAM	18
FARNHAM	27
Farley Chamberlayne	6
Farnborough Station	33
Freefolk and Laverstoke ...	14
GOSPORT	24
Grately	18
Hambledon	18
HAVANT	28
Herriard	23
Hinton Ampner	9
Houghton (2 miles from Stockbridge)	11
Hunton	9
Hursley	5
Hurstbourne Priors	12
Itchen Abbas	5
Itchen Stoke	6
Kilmiston	8
Kingsomborne	9
Leckford	9
Littleton...	3
Longparish	10
LONDON, by Farnham ...	67
,, by Basingstoke ...	63
Ludgershall	20
Medstead	15
Meonstoke	14
Micheldever (Station) ...	10
Micheldever (Village)	7
Michelmersh	12
Monk Sherborne	23
Morestead	4
NEWBURY	24
Nutley	15
ODIHAM	28
Otterbourne	4
Overton	14
Ovington	6
Owslebury	5
OXFORD	53
PETERSFIELD	18
Popham Lane	12
PORTSMOUTH	27
Privett	13
READING	34
RINGWOOD	29
ROMSEY	11
Ropley	11
SALISBURY	25
SOUTHAMPTON	12
Sparsholt	4
Steventon	14
Stockbridge	9
Stoke Charity	8
Stoneham, North	8
Stratton, East	8
Swarraton	9
Tichborne	8
Tisted, West	13
Tunworth	15
Twyford	4
Upham	9
Warnford	11
Westmeon	12
Weyhill	17
Wherwell	10
WHITCHURCH	12
Wickham	14
Winchfield	27
Wonston	7
Woodmancote	11
Worthy, Headbourne	2
Worthy, King's	3
Worthy, Martyr	4
Worting	17
Wyke	1

LIST OF BISHOPS.

Those marked with an asterisk are *not* buried in the Cathedral.

Birinus—died A.D. 650
*Ægilberht—resigned 662, afterwards Bishop of Paris
*Wini—ejected 666; died Bishop of London
*Eleutherius—died 676
*Hedda—died 705
Daniel—resigned 744, died 745
*Hunferth—died 754
*Cyneheard
*Æthelard—translated to Dover 790
Ecgbald—living in 793
Dudda—793
Cyneberht—779
Alhmund—803
Wigthegen—died ante 824
Hereferth—died 883
Edmund
Helmstan—died 852
Swithun—died 862
*Alhferth—translated to Canterbury 871, died 889
*Dunbert—died 879
Denewulf—died 909
*Frithstan—resigned 931, died 932
Brynstan—died 934
*Ælfhead the Bald—died 951
*Ælfsyne—nominated to Canterbury 958, died 961
*Brithelm—died 963
*Æthelwold—died 984
*Elphege—translated to Canterbury 1005, died 1012
Kenulf—died 1006
Æthelwold II.—died 1015
*Ælfsige—died 1032
Alwyn—died 1047
Stigand—translated to Canterbury 1052, died 1070
Walkelyn—died 1098
William Giffard—died 1128–9
Henry de Blois—died 1171
Richard Toclyve—died 1189
Godfrey de Lucy—died 1204
Peter de la Roche—died 1238
*William Raleigh—died 1250
Ethelmar—died 1261
*John Grevase, alias John of Exon—died 1268
Nicholas Ely—died 1280
John Sawbridge, or de Pontissarra, died 1304
Henry Woodlock—died 1316
*John Sandale—died 1319
*Reginald Asser—died 1323
*John Stratford—translated to Canterbury 1333, died 1348
Adam Orlton—1345
William Edyngton—died 1366
William Wykeham—died 1404
Henry Beaufort—died 1447
William Wayneflete—died 1486
*Peter Courtenay—died 1492
Thomas Langton—died 1500
Richard Fox—died 1528
*Thomas Wolsey—died 1530
Stephen Gardiner—deprived 1550, restored 1553, died 1555
*John Poynet—deprived 1553, died 1556
John White—deprived 1559, died 1559-60
*Robert Horne—died 1580
John Watson—died 1583
Thomas Cooper—died 1594
*William Wickham II—died 1595
*William Day—1596
*Thomas Bilson—1616
*James Montague—1618
*Lancelot Andrewes—1626
*Richard Neile—translated to York 1632, died 1640
*Walter Curle—died 1647 or 1650
*Bryan Duppa—died 1662
George Morley—died 1684
Peter Mews—1706
*Sir J. Trelawny, Bart.—died 1721
Charles Trimnell—died 1723
Richard Willis—died 1734
Benjamin Hoadly—died 1761
John Thomas—died 1781
Hon. Brownlow North—died 1820
Sir G. P. Tomline, Bt.—died 1827
*Charles R. Sumner—resigned 1869, died 1874
*Samuel Wilberforce—died 1873
*Edward Harold Browne

LIST OF MAYORS.

Florence de Lunn A.D. 1184
Ditto 85
Ralph de Mullings
Philip Lubin
Roger de Ingepen
Laurence de Lunn
John le Cross 90
Ditto
Ditto
Peter de Flitchley
Peter Lubin
Ade de Cheriton 95
Roger de Long
Edward de Draper
John Gabriell
Ade de Cloiffe
Ralph Francis 1200
Philip Lubin
Nich. de Mullings
Edward de Draper
Nich. Gabriell
Nich. de Exton 5
John de Hockley
John de Lunn
Robert de Froyle
John de Hockley
Jeffery de Ring 10
Edward de Draper
John de Royle
Jeffery att Lamden
Richard Fry
William Attbolme 15
John de Mande
Marke de Ring
Ade de Burnett
Marke Delaroone
Ralph de Milner 20
Robert de Froyle
Thomas de Slayden
Roger le Canacre
John de Wareham
W. de Mitcheldever 25
John de Pelbar
Ralph le Spicer
John Terrill
William Winsflud
Walter Chamberlain 30
Stephen Tisteed
John Blake
Nich. de Exton
Walter Delaroone.
Roger de Long 35
Ade de Kilmeston
John le Sherfield
Florence le Grasse
Laurence de Luce
Garr. de Sparkford 40
Ralph de Sheffield
Hugh le Weaver
Philip Lubin

Thomas Attzard 1244
Robert Attrooke 45
Roger de Winsflud
Nich. de Devenish
John Attbrad
Ralph Clavell
Nich. de Sherfield 50
Jeffery de Wareham
William Morraine
J. de Mitcheldever
Roger de Winsflud
W. le Harrington 55
Robert de Franfoide
Marke le Weaver
John Ingepen
Garret Marleborough
Laurence de Blaine 60
Nich. Luben
Jeffery Delaroone
Hugh le Crosse
Walter de Nicholas
Hugh le Sparkford 65
Ade de Froyle
Marke de Draper
Robert le Irenmonger
Nich. de King
Marke de Flitchley 70
Ade de Exton
Richard Davenish
Jeffery de Froyle
Math. de Bollenden
Roger de Long 75
Ralph Francis
Garret de Issington
Ralph de Hockley
William de Wodere
Henry Jordan 80
William de Parnfold
William de Nortley
Nich. le Devenish
John Wickon
Stephen le Weeke 85
Reynard Wigg
Ralph de Mullins
William le Mercer
William de Wareham
John de Hannyton 90
John Spragg
Henry Wickby
Stephen Crane
Stephen att Lamden
Walter de Vayre 95
Raynard Read
William de Mullings
Jerman Hardy
John Clavell
Raymond Wilson 1300
Walter de Hill
Thomas Bickton
Thomas Jerman

Walter Bolt 1304
Ralph Francis 5
John de Hockley
Robert de Sherfield
John de Exton
Robert de Farnfold
Walter le Fox 10
Ralph de Hannyton
John le Devenish
John Patchford
Rich. le Devenish
J. de Mitcheldever 15
John Parnfold
Thomas le Mayne
Laurence le Weeke
Thomas Smith
Walter Chandlier 20
Rich. Chamberlain
John Spragg
John Copping
John Browne
Nich. le Devenish 25
Robert Foster
Laurence le Fox
John le March
Leonard Taylor
John le Grasse 30
John de Nicholl
Nich. de Exton
John de Hockley
Ralph de Mullings
John Gabriell 35
Robert de Farnfold
Ralph de Mullings
John Gabriell
Nich. le Devenish
Ditto 40
John Gabriell
John Lumen Draper
Nich. de Exton
W. de Mitcheldever
W. de Parnfold 45
Jeffery att Lambden
W. de Mitcheldever
John Russell
John de Nortley
Stephen de Fox 50
William de Winsflud
Walter Chamberlain
Nich. de Hannyton
John Wickley
Ralph Attchurch 55
Henry Read
Stephen Hayne
Hugh le Crane
Ralph de Mullings
William Haselwood 60
Thomas le Spicer
Nich. de Hannyton
Stephen Hayne

LIST OF MAYORS—*Continued.*

Name	Year
Richard Wigg	1364
John Bickton	65
Hugh le Crane	
William Jugg	
John Bett	
Walter Boles	
Hugh Crane	70
Ralph Ford	
Richard Wigg	
Richard le Frye	
John att Zerd	
William Jugg	75
John Bett	
John Devenish	
Jerman Fardy	
John Haywood	
Ditto	80
Richard Frye	
Richard Wigg	
Robert Mayhew	
Wm. Jugg	
John Blake	85
Wm. Castle	
Walter Boles	
Richard Clavell	
Richard Chamberlain	
Robert Attrooke	90
Wm. Mourym	
Wm. Wigg	
Wm. Jugg	
Robert Attrooke	
John Blake	95
Wm. Wigg	
Wm. Bolter	
Gilbert Foster	
Thomas Smith	
Marke le Fayre	1400
Ditto	
Thomas Smith	
Edward Pickard	
Mark le Fayre	
John Blake	5
Gilbert Foster	
Wm. Bolt	
Wm. Wigg	
John Blake	
Marke le Fayre	10
John Bayley	
John Attoke	
Marke le Fayre	
Wm. West	
Thomas Veale	15
Wm. Esteed	
John Jourdain	
John Attoke	
Richard Bolt	
Richard Turnant	20
Thomas Sutton	
Wm. Reason	
John Veale	
John Summerford	
John Summerford	1425
Walter Hoare	
Richard Turnant	
John Blake	
John Bye	
John West	30
Wm. Sutton	
Thomas Froyle	
Richard de Warmburge	
Thomas Lacy	
Robert Hooper	35
Robert Hockley	
John Smith	
Wm. Hoar	
John Clavell	
Robert Foster	40
William Goffe	
Thomas Harvye	
Thomas Attrooke	
Wm. Bett	
John West	45
John Randye	
Thomas Hoimes	
Thomas Plaine	
Thomas Froyle	
Thomas Poole	50
Wm. Ford	
Wm. Attoake	
Thomas Blake	
John Woole	
Thomas Jordaine	55
John Warner	
Gilbert Blake	
John Spicer	
John Attchurch	
John Wigg	60
Philip Ring	
John Gater	
John Tanner	
Wm. Chase	
Thomas Harvey	65
John Bednam	
John Terrill	
John Lacy	
John Pratt	
Wm. Blake	70
John Jugg	
John Mitcheldever	
John Hayne	
Wm. Holt	
Thomas Reason	75
John Froyle	
John Foster	
John Collins	
Wm. Chandelie	
Thomas Thorne	80
John Shelden	
John Brown	
Richard Bolt	
John Bramdine	
John Calcroft	85
Richard Butler	1486
Stephen Bramdens	
Roger Wilde	
Richard Bull	
Nicholas Biggs	90
John Stratford	
John Gander	
John Stocker	
Stephen Bramdeane	
Simon Finch	95
John Beedle	
John Calcrosse	
John Wheeler	
John Blake	
John Stratford	1500
Richard Biggs	
Thomas Colvill	
Ditto	
John Gander	
Walter Wood	5
John Litchfield	
John Bellingham	
John Butler	
John Bird	
John Butler	10
John Bellingham	
Thomas Clarke	
John Webb	
Adam Watts	
Thomas Baker	15
Thomas Hayne	
John Butler	
Wm. Jennings	
John Bellingham	
Thomas Webb	20
Thomas Baker	
Thomas Vincent	
Peter Bird	
Wm. Gryme	
John Lawrance	25
John Butler	
John Bellingham	
Thomas Webb	
Adam Watts	
Walter Williamson	30
Walter Chandelier	
John Laurance	
Thomas Lurkin	
John Skillicorne	
Robert Badger	35
Thomas Vincent	
John Hall	
Wm. Farringdon	
John Godfrey	
Edmund Foster	40
John Skillicorne	
Robert Badger	
John Hall	
Arthur Robbye	
Robert Hodson	45
Gilbert Laurance	

LIST OF MAYORS—*Continued.*

Stephen Bedham 1547
Wm. Lawrance
Edmund Foster
John Edmunds 50
Robert Hodson
Robert Beathell
Wm. Lawrance
Ditto
Robert Bethell 55
John Edmunds
Giles White
Wm. Godwin
Richard Burton
John Skinner 60
Thomas Bath
Thomas Colly
Wm. Lane
Robert Hodson
John White 65
Wm. Hall
John Edmunds
Richard Burton
John Skinner
Wm. Lane 70
Richard Bird
Wm. Badger
Stephen Ashton
Wm. Lawrance
Wm. Simonds 75
Wm. Hall
Richard Bird
Wm. Bethell
Richard Cooke
Ditto 80
Wm. Hudson
Anthony Bird
John White
Richard Bird
Wm. Symonds 85
Wm. Badger
Edward Cole
Charles Newbolt
John Paice
Wm. Hodson 90
Richard Cooke
John Luke
John White
Wm. Beacham
Richard Emery 95
Wm. Symonds
Wm. Badger
Edward Cole
Anthony Bird
Charles Newbolt 1600
Richard Cooke
Wm. Hodson
Wm. Beacham
Richard Adderly
John Luke 5
George Pemerton
Simon Barksdale

Thomas Bedham 1608
Christopher Hussey
Wm. Budd 10
Thomas Child
Edward Cole
Edward White
Richard Adderly
Lancelott Thorpe 15
George Pemerton
Simon Barksdale
Christopher Hussey
Wm. Budd
Thomas Child 20
Edward White
Wm. Longland
Lancelott Thorpe
John Trussell
John Lamphiere 25
Edward Cole
Martin Yalden
Thomas Godson
Ralph Riggs
Wm. Longland 30
Christopher Hussey
Edward White
John Trussell
Martin Yaldes
Thomas Godson 35
Ralph Riggs
Robert Toocker
Wm. Hancock
Joseph Butler
Edward White 40
Wm. Longland
Thomas Godson
Richard Braxtone
Wm. Longland
Ralph Riggs 45
Robert Matthews
Edward White
Joseph Butler
Edmund Riggs
Thomas Muspratt 50
John Champion
Edward Hooker
Wm. Harwood
Edmund Riggs
Nich. Purdue 55
Richard Dennett
Thomas Muspratt
John Champion
Edmund Fyfield
John Munday 60
James Guy
John Colson
Benjamin Clarke
Wm. Taylor
Nich. Purdue 65
Richard Dennett
Edmund Fyfield
Thomas Muspratt

Wm. Craddock 1669
Wm. Smith 70
Thomas Wavell
Benjamin Clarke
Wm. Taylor
Anthony Yalden
Godson Penton 75
John Warner
Edmund Fyfield
Wm. Craddock
Thomas Wavell
Benjamin Clarke }
Wm. Taylor } 80
Thomas Coward
Anthony Yalden
Godson Penton
John Warner
Ellis Mews 85
James Earle
Thomas Wavell
Ditto
Thomas Pink
Matthew Imber 90
James Barfoote
John Purdue
Richard Good
Henry Sharpe
Wm. Over 95
Godson Penton
Thomas Cropp
John Perdue, sen.
Richard Good
Matthew Imber 1700
Henry Sharpe
Thomas Cropp
John Blake
David Wavell
John Penton 5
John Perdue, sen.
Richard Smith
John Soane
Thomas Cropp
David Wavell 10
Robert Clarke
Matthew Imber
Thomas Merriott
John Blake
Edward Hooker 15
Gilbert Wavell
Richard Gosnell }
Gilbert Wavell } 17
John Foyle
Thomas Coward
Edward Hooker 20
John Foyle
Thomas Barfoote
Matthew Imber
Thomas Barfoote
Thomas Godwin 25
John Foyle
Thomas Barfoote

LIST OF MAYORS—*Continued.*

Robert Waldron 1728
Matthew Imber
Wm. Spearing 30
Wm. Waldron
Robert Waldron
Samuel Smith
Wm. Waldron
Wm. Spearing 35
Thomas Barfoote
Gilbert Wavill
Jacob Gater
Thomas Barfoote
John Gauntlet 40
Thomas Waldron
Wm. Waldron
Thomas Barfoote
Thomas Waldron
Samuel Smith 45
Wm. Olding
Wm. Waldron
Jacob Gater
Nich. Perdue Smith
Arthur Good 50
Harry Green, sen.
Daniel Lashford
Thomas Waldron
Wm. Waldron
Nich. Perdue Smith 55
Wm. Prior
James Spearing
Berrington King
George Durnford
Henry Penton 60
His Grace, Charles, Duke of Bolton
James Spearing
John Wool
Berrington King
George Durnford 65
James White
N. P. Smith
George Durnford
John Dyson
Henry Penton 70
Sir Paulet St. John
William Knapp
His Grace the Duke of Chandos
Thomas Waldron } 74
His Grace the Duke of Chandos } 74
James Spearing 75
Harry Green
John Doswell

James White 1778
George Durnford
William Knapp 80
John Doswell
James White
George Durnford
His Grace the Duke of Chandos
Sir Wm. Hillman 85
Joseph Barker
John Doswell
James White
George Durnford
George Earle 90
Richard Gamon
John N. Silver
John Ridding
Richard H. Lloyd
George Earle 95
John N. Silver
John Mant
Sir Henry Paulet St. John Mildmay
Joseph Barker
George Earle 1800
John N. Silver
John Clerk
Joseph Barker
George Earle
John N. Silver 5
John Mant
Joseph Barker }
John Mant }
Sir H. C. St. John Mildmay
John N. Silver 10
William Druitt
John Meare
Richard Henry Lloyd
William Cave, jun.
John N. Silver 15
Wm. Druitt
Wm. Barnes
John Mant
Paulet St. John Mildmay
Earl Temple 20
John N. Silver
Wm. Barnes
John Mant
Richard Littlehales
Giles K. Lyford 25
Wm. Barnes
John Mant
Richard Littlehales

John Earle 1829
Giles K. Lyford 30
Wm. Barnes
John Earle
George Wm. Chard
Charles W. Benny
John Young 35
Ditto *
Ditto
John V. Earle
John Parmiter
Charles Mayo 40
Charles Wooldridge
Wm. Whitear Bulpett
Charles Wittman Benny
Charles Seagrim
Charles Mayo 45
Henry Barnes
C. Ruby Thomas
Charles Seagrim
C. March Deane
Ed. C. Faithfull 50
Charles Seagrim
Charles Mayo
Wm. Barrow-Simonds
Charles Robey Rogers
John Ventham 55
Charles Wright
Ditto
Joseph Dowling
Wm. Hutchinson
John Naish 60
Charles Wooldridge
Charles Wright
Wm. Forder
Thomas Waters
Wm. Budden 65
Ditto
Charles Fielder
Sharp St. John Butt
Harry Wm. Kelsey
Robert Underwood 70
Charles Warner
Robert P. Forder
Frederick Morshead
Wm. Budden
Charles Fielder 75
Frederick Morshead
Thomas Stopher
John Thomas Clifton
John Croft Moore
Cornelius John Drew 80
Edward Douglas Godwin

* First Mayor elected under the Municipal Reform Act.

THE CHAIN WORN BY THE MAYOR DURING HIS YEAR OF OFFICE.—This Chain was presented by the citizens in the year 1879. It is of 18-carat gold, the style Early Gothic. The badge is circular, having the arms of the City, the five castles in silver, and two lions in gold, relieved by red enamelled ground, with Gothic diaper. The arms are surrounded by Gothic tracery and a rich border of flowers, having in the centre sapphires set *en cabochon*, alternated with enamelled letters, which form the name of the City. The centre link is a cinquefoil, adorned with English roses, and a mediæval representation of Henry II giving the charter to the City, in A.D. 1184. The legend is 'Henry II, civibus Winton.' As supporters to the central badge, and to the quatrefoils round the chain, are eight massive lions, with red tongues and emerald eyes. These are finely modelled. Four of the quatrefoils, placed at intervals round the chain, contain shields finely emblazoned. One is the armorial bearings of the Bishopric; another the paternal shield of Paulet, Marquis of Winchester; a third the arms of William of Wykeham; lastly, the arms of St. Cross, which has retained its original character through all the vicissitudes of 740 years. Others bear the City castles, having two subsidiary ornaments each with two castles, making two groups of five castles each side of the chain.

Warren and Son, Printers and Publishers, 85, High Street.

www.ingramcontent.com/pod-product-compliance
Ingram Content Group UK Ltd.
Pitfield, Milton Keynes, MK11 3LW, UK
UKHW021347100326
11180UKWH00021B/1411

9 781024 435504